I0125759

Foreign Direct Investment, Democracy, and Development

The effects of globalization on economy and society are highly contested subjects in academic and political arenas. This study brings an empirical perspective to the crucially important arguments that encapsulate the major debates in this area. Is globalization a path to prosperity, an urgent necessity for the large majority of this world's citizens who are too poor to debate theory? Is neoliberal optimism justified given the serious challenges that internationalization of an economy is supposed to pose to local economies and societies? Using quantitative data, this book addresses the shape and degree of internationalization by focusing on the impact of foreign direct investment (FDI) and democracy on economic development and the effects of economic internationalization on democracy.

The author's results suggest that we are wrong in overemphasizing a contradiction between economic internationalization and democratization. By addressing the influential research tradition within sociology and political science that sees the structural power of international capitalism as exploitative and thereby harmful to developing countries, the author demonstrates that globalization does benefit the poorer states and that such states are not as globalized as polemical arguments claim. The author examines democracy's effects on economic growth and considers the claim that foreign capital has a detrimental effect on democracy to show that FDI in fact plays a supporting role for democracy and creates higher growth rates than domestic capital. From these results the author suggests that policymakers should seek to encourage globalization by ensuring open access to products from poorer countries and encouraging private investment within poorer countries, and that such countries should concentrate on building up human and institutional capital to attract investment.

Foreign Direct Investment, Democracy, and Development will be essential reading for academics and advanced students within the fields of political science, sociology, development studies, and economics.

Indra de Soysa is Senior Research Fellow at the Center for Development Research, University of Bonn, Germany, and leads a research group on "Democracy, Rule of Law, and Governance." He has recently published articles in the *Journal of Conflict Resolution*, *American Sociological Review*, the *Journal of Peace Research*, and *Global Environmental Politics*, and a number of book chapters in edited volumes. His research primarily centers on such issues as democratization, political economy of violence, and the effects of globalization on the economy and society.

Routledge Advances in International Political Economy

Foreign Direct Investment, Democracy, and Development

Assessing contours, correlates, and concomitants of globalization

Indra de Soysa

Routledge
Taylor & Francis Group

LONDON AND NEW YORK

First published 2003 by Routledge
2 Park Square, Milton Park, Abingdon, Oxfordshire OX14 4RN

Simultaneously published in the USA and Canada by Routledge
711 Third Avenue, New York, NY 10017

First issued in paperback 2014

Routledge is an imprint of the Taylor and Francis Group, an informa business

Transferred to Digital Printing 2005

© 2003 Indra de Soysa

Typeset in Sabon by The Running Head Limited, Cambridge

All rights reserved. No part of this book may be reprinted
or reproduced or utilized in any form or by any electronic,
mechanical, or other means, now known or hereafter
invented, including photocopying and recording, or in any
information storage or retrieval system, without permission
in writing from the publishers.

British Library Cataloguing in Publication Data
A catalogue record for this book is available from the British Library

Library of Congress Cataloging in Publication Data
de Soysa, Indra.
Foreign direct investment, democracy, and development: assessing contours, correlates,
and concomitants of globalization / Indra de Soysa.
p. cm.
Includes bibliographical references and index.
1. Investments, Foreign. 2. International trade. 3. International economic integration.
4. Investments, Foreign—Developing countries. 5. Developing countries—Economic
conditions—21st century. 6. Globalization—Economic aspects—Developing countries.
7. Globalization—Social aspects—Developing countries. 8. Democracy—Developing
countries.
I. Title.

HG4538 .D37 2003
337—dc21   2002036935

ISBN 978-0-415-25054-2 (hbk)
ISBN 978-1-138-81074-7 (pbk)

I dedicate this book to the memory of my father, Victor Charles de Soysa, who supported all our "harebrained schemes." He would have been proud of this!

Contents

Figures

Tables

Acknowledgments

This book began in the early 1990s when "globalization" was being discussed under other theoretical guises. Therefore, it is well placed to evaluate what is old and new about the debates and the empirical realities that have unfolded during the past decade. I owe a deep debt of gratitude to John Oneal, a mentor and friend, for introducing me to the subject and urging me to look beyond the polemics and "let the data speak." I continue to learn from John. Several people have helped in numerous ways over the years, particularly Tatu Vanhanen, who freely shared data and thoughts, and Glenn Firebaugh and Rajneesh Narula for encouraging comments at an early stage. I am grateful to have been able to collaborate with Nils Petter Gleditsch, whose contributions are manifest throughout the book. I am particularly indebted to Ross Burkhart for his help with making the manuscript better. A host of people offered generous comments at varying stages. I am grateful to Arend Lijphart, Erich Weede, Witold Henisz, Scott Gates, Haavard Hegre, Anke Hoeffler, Peter Wehrheim, Carsten Burhop, Suzanna Wolf, and several other colleagues at Zentrum für Entwicklungs Forschung (Center for Development Research) for insightful comments and suggestions. They are not to blame for remaining errors of commission and omission. I thank Maria Lensu and Angelika Wagner for invaluable help with preparing the manuscript. Finally, I owe an enormous debt to my wife, Ann Kristin, who sacrifices a lot for the "family business" during my time away from home. The "business of the family," our daughters Sooriya Anne and Christiane Devika, will remain puzzled for some time as to why "Herr Dr. de Soysa" cannot cure people. I sincerely hope that at least a tiny portion of what is contained within might be "medicine"—even if for insomnia!

Abbreviations

APEC	Asia Pacific Economic Cooperation
ASEAN	Association of South East Asian Nations
ATTAC	Taxation of Financial Transaction for the Aid of Citizens (translated from the French)
EU	European Union
FDI	foreign direct investment
FPE	final prediction error
GATT	General Agreement on Tariffs and Trade
GDN	Global Development Network
GDP	gross domestic product
GNP	gross national product
IMF	International Monetary Fund
ISI	import substitution industrialization
LDCs	least developed countries
MAI	Multilateral Agreement on Investment
Mercosur	Mercado Común del Sur (Common Market of the South)
MPR	military participation ratio
MNCs	multinational corporations
NAFTA	North American Free Trade Agreement
NICs	newly industrialized countries
OECD	Organization for Economic Cooperation and Development
PEN	(foreign capital) penetration
PPP	purchasing power parity
PR	proportional representation
SMP	single member plurality
SSA	sub-Saharan Africa
UN	United Nations
UNCTAD	United Nations Conference on Trade and Development
UNDP	United Nations Development Programme
UNICEF	United Nations Children's Fund
UNRISD	United Nations Research Institute for Social Development
WTO	World Trade Organization

Introduction

Even the skeptics, who doubt the meaningfulness of the term "globalization," are forced to admit that expectations surrounding it—from Mongolia to Managua—are high. It is *the* word on everyone's lips. Globalization is, according to some, the "defining characteristic of our time" (Adams *et al.*, 1999: 1). Others deem it the "most pressing issue" facing society today (Stiglitz, 2002: 4). This study's principal task is to bring some empirical perspective to basic but crucially important arguments that encapsulate the major debates on the subject—is globalization a path to prosperity, an urgent necessity for the large majority of this world's citizens who are too poor to debate theory? Is neoliberal optimism justified given the serious challenges that internationalization of an economy is supposed to pose to local economies and societies? This book addresses the question of global economic integration and economic and political development by focusing on the three most salient integrative forces driving globalization—the spread of MNCs, trade, and the simultaneous spread of democracy.

In the economic sphere it is trade and FDI that are driving economic integration, binding states and societies in an ever-tighter web of interdependence (Sachs and Warner, 1995a; Dunning and Hamdani, 1997; Birdsall and Lawrence, 1999; Mittelman, 2000; Nye and Donahue, 2000).[1] This aspect of globalization is anathema for many—economic liberalization across the world is simply allowing corporate greed to plunder poor societies, and the web of interdependence is in reality "a global trap" meant for the poor (Martin and Schumann, 1997; Falk, 1999). Globalization, or what some see as an intensified phase of the internationalization of capitalism, apparently poses serious contradictions (Armijo, 1999a; Munck and Gills, 2002).

Two camps have formed on the issue of globalization—pessimists and optimists. The pessimists make up an amorphous coalition of interests that are made up of economic nationalists, such as Jean-Marie Le Pen in France and Ross Perot in the US, who would like to protect national enterprises from foreign competition. Mixed in are activists of many sorts, concerned about issues such as environmental degradation, fair trade, global corporate accountability, human rights, and groups concerned about the role of the multilateral lending institutions, such the IMF and World Bank which are accused of unfairly "adjusting" the macroenvironments of poor countries so as to make them more receptive to liberal free market conditions. Mixed in within this broad group are fringe groups such as anarchists and religious fundamentalists. It is not surprising that the coherence of some of the arguments are severely compromised because they are aimed at globalization broadly, but it is not unfair to characterize many of the concerns as revolving around the structural power of MNCs and their expected effects on poor societies.

This study addresses the concerns of objectors referred to by some as "communitarians," who generally see trade and FDI as exploiting poor countries (Gilpin, 2000). They call for better "governance" of globalization, requiring that it be "managed" better. Some orthodox economists, such as Joseph Stiglitz and Dani Rodrik, lend credence to concerns that globalization is really not reflecting the interests of the poor, but that broad-based liberalization only serves to marginalize poor countries, even if both these scholars are positive about globalization's potential role in raising welfare. According to Stiglitz (2002: 4), "opening up to international trade has helped many countries grow far more quickly than they would otherwise have."

Stiglitz's major contention, however, is with the policies that are pushed by multilateral agencies, particularly the IMF, who he sees as pandering to vested interests in Washington and the major capitals. In other words, the multilateral agencies are guilty of managing globalization for the benefit of the powerful and not in the service of the needy. This is undoubtedly true, and noisy protest in the West affects Western leaders concerned about their own narrow constituencies—unskilled workers, farmers, etc.[2] Without touching the heat of policy debates concerning what the West's policies for solving the problems of poor countries should be, this study merely looks at the objective outcomes of globalization in terms of growth and the sustainability of democracy, relating the current debates to earlier theoretical and empirical work on the effects of the structure of a global capitalist system on poor countries. In other words, this study will examine the concerns raised by the discontented in terms of previously debated theoretical concerns and empirical realities.

FDI and trade are widely regarded as pillars of economic globalization. In the sociopolitical sphere an unprecedented number of states have yielded to the "third wave" of democratization, opening up processes of "localization" where Cold War imperatives had previously imposed superpower "solutions" to localized, often homegrown problems requiring homegrown solutions. In fact, Cold War stability in much of the Third World came in the form of repression, promoted and supported by one or the other side in the superpower game (Huntington, 1991). This game has changed. As the superpower-dominated bloc politics recedes, increasing liberalization of markets is happening apace with increasing levels of participation of people in national political life, empowered by the formal trappings of "democracy." As one scholar has written, "Underlying the present global transformation, there seem to be forces that are generating fundamental changes on two dimensions—toward internationalization and democratization" (Sakamoto, 1994: 1). Supporters of globalization are liable to see the processes of democratization and liberalization of economies as coterminous—an optimistic sign for building a better future. Liberalization of markets and spreading democracy are conducive to peace, a proposition that goes back to ancient times, but is articulated most precisely by Montesquieu, Immanuel Kant, and the Manchester School (Russett and Oneal, 2000). Opponents of globalization are less sanguine. Given the predatory nature of globalization, they see no future for increasing economic welfare, or sustaining newfound liberty and peace (Armijo, 1999b; Munck, 2002).[3] This book is largely devoted to addressing the theoretical and empirical foundations of the optimistic and pessimistic outlooks on globalization and development.

This study addresses the effects of FDI and political democracy on economic development in an integrated manner. It examines the latest data and propositions, testing theoretically precise hypotheses. It is hoped that the results contribute to the debates on the potential of global integration for alleviating poverty and sustaining democracy in the developing world and push theory building forward based on empirical realities. Globalization is a subject on which much polemical discussion and journalistic, anecdotal evidence is paraded as fact, with ample use of hyperbole. However, as some scholars urge, the "real-world implications" of economic deprivation require social scientists to muster the best evidence and make only the most scientific inferences to insure that policy takes into account the certainties and uncertainties reflected in the empirical evidence (King *et al.*, 1994).

This study focuses on debates on globalization within the fields of political science, sociology, development studies, and economics. Since the 1999 WTO conference in Seattle, the galvanization of an antiglobalization movement that has taken its cause(s) to the streets signifies the depth of discontent among some, particularly in the West. A reverse wave of globalization today is much less fantasy compared with the optimism following the heady days of collapsing communism, when scholars could even proclaim the "end of history" (Fukuyama, 1991). Globalizing waves followed by periods of backwash, after all, have been the pattern of integration and division in the modern state system (World Bank, 2002a), and close scrutiny of 19th-century globalization shows how fragile the process can be (O'Rourke and Williamson, 1999), leading many to invoke the famous Polanyian argument of a "double movement," or the social reaction that seeks to tame the expansion of market forces. Apparently, the current discontent on the streets is a manifestation of the double movement seeking to tame the market (Hettne, 2002; Munck, 2002).

Why should democracy and foreign capital be studied as important determinants of the future of global integration? According to the optimistic outlook on global integration, the degree of liberalization on *both* politics and economics is crucial for evaluating its future. The current phase of globalization comes with comparatively little direct political domination given the end of formal colonialism, or the imperial control of the vast majority of people by a handful of powerful states, as was the case in the 19th century. Liberal economics and politics, signified by the spread of sovereign states and democracy, are the norm today. For the pessimists the trend of integration, fueled by liberal economic imperatives, is foreboding, both for economic progress and for the sustainability of democracy within poor states (Gill, 1997; Mittelman, 1997; Armijo, 1999a).[4] For the pessimists, globalization and liberalization are the intensification of predatory processes (Falk, 1999). The bulk of the debate on globalization and development, as it plays out in the social sciences, particularly in political science, sociology, and development studies, has been rather polemical where sweeping statements are made based largely on anecdotal evidence. Very little systematic evidence exists that persuades either way, which is particularly true of development studies, which straddles several social science disciplines. As one prominent scholar has remarked, however, "In no other field of the social sciences are politics and economics so closely intertwined as in the study of development . . . Economists studying developing societies rarely train in political science, while political scientists too often remain unschooled in economics" (Bates, 1988: 1).

This study contributes to this debate by combining the empirical and theoretical work from both economics and the "other social sciences" by testing theoretically informed hypotheses arising from the questions raised by globalization. I particularly focus on the question of FDI and democracy and economic development and questions relating democracy to globalization—"a major issue of the day" (Munck, 2002: 11). The study highlights the latest theoretical and empirical knowledge on the subject of FDI and growth and of democracy and growth within the fields of economics, political science and sociology. It provides new empirical analyses and theoretical perspectives and utilizes the most recent data on FDI, examining a longer span of time than previously examined in similar studies. The study offers novel ways of thinking about the question of democratization and economic growth, pushing the research in new directions.

The study addresses empirical evidence that helped to forge a strong consensus, which sees democracy as unnecessary for growth (Barro, 1998; Przeworski *et al.*, 2000). I show that these analyses, largely emanating from economics, have generally used subjective indices of democracy in their empirical analyses in ways that do not capture qualitative aspects of democracy that are linked theoretically to economic growth and have normative implications for the ways in which we think about democracy. I demonstrate that the null results on democracy and growth are largely a function of the gap between the conceptualization of democracy and the measures used in the operationalization. The standard measures of democracy conflate aspects of democracy important for growth with those that may in fact be harmful, because most measures contain various subjective aspects about democracy that do not fit very well with democratic theory. This study brings the discussions on democracy and growth closer to democratic theory and tests several theoretically defined hypotheses. Understanding the correlates and concomitants of globalization by taking FDI and democracy seriously is one crucial way of getting at the heart of whether or not liberalization and democratization clash. In other words, what is to be expected from "the symbiotic antagonism," to use Robert Dahl's (2000) expression, between the market and democracy, for improving conditions in the poor world? Addressing this question is the principal task of this book.

Outline of study

First, the study examines the effects of FDI on economic growth. I specifically address the influential research tradition within sociology and political science that sees the structural power of international capitalism as exploitative and thereby harmful to developing countries, arguments mirrored in the current debate on globalization. I focus particularly on the empirical evidence generated by a large body of literature spearheaded by the work of sociologists Volker Bornschier and Christopher Chase-Dunn (1985), which report that the "penetration" of MNCs of the poor economies is likely to systematically underdevelop these states politically, socially, and economically. I address the controversies surrounding the findings and interpretations of this influential body of research, which have come to dominate discussions in sociology and political science. Using the previous theoretical and empirical studies as a backdrop, this study tests theory-based, policy-relevant issues with new data.

Second, the study examines democracy's effects on economic growth. Since it has been argued that MNC investments have a heavy bearing on the initiation and sustainability of democracy, and since the optimistic outlook on globalization views these two factors to be propitious, this study integrates both factors in its analyses. Do, for example, large inflows of FDI to authoritarian states, such as the People's Republic of China, compensate for the lack of democracy, given FDI's supposed affinity to political stability? Such an argument has been made explicitly on the issue of corruption and growth, but this question is neglected in most models identifying the sources of democratic development. First, however, the theoretical issues of democracy and growth are closely considered, and particular attention is paid to recent empirical analyses. This study also addresses the structuralist's claim that foreign capital has a detrimental effect on democracy. While I pay careful attention to theory-based arguments, I fundamentally focus on empirical evidence, making empirical tests that would allow me to evaluate theory and current policy debates.

The book is organized as follows: this Introduction is followed by a discussion of the general debates surrounding the issue of globalization. I examine its contours and empirical trends reflected in the data. Chapter 2 connects the discussions on globalization with older theories of development and underdevelopment, largely the dependency and world-systems research traditions, examining what is stale and what is novel about the arguments in the new debates on globalization. Chapter 3 focuses on the empirical realities and new tests on the issue of FDI and economic growth. Chapter 4 tackles the question of democracy and development and presents the theoretical propositions to be tested. Chapter 5 tests democracy and growth issues and the issue of democracy and FDI. Chapter 6 summarizes the results and examines implications for policy.

1   The contours of globalization

The globalization debate

Globalization is currently *the* catchphrase for the perils and promises facing humanity in the 21st century (Giddens, 1999; Gilpin, 2000; Held and McGrew, 2000; Nye and Donahue, 2000).[1] Globalization is generally understood as economic, political, and social integration of states and societies, both horizontally and vertically, in tighter webs of interdependence. Globalization is a *process* and not a qualitatively different endstate, where politics and the state have become superfluous and the market has taken over. Horizontal and vertical integration of states in the global economy is currently taking place through at least two major visible and measurable processes—the rapid spread of foreign capital, trade, and the spread of the ideas of political democracy and market principles to an extent never before witnessed in modern history. The debate on the desirability of globalization takes place between those who see this trend as mutually beneficial and those who see this as the intensification of exploitation by the so-called international capitalist forces exemplified by global transnational corporations. Most governments in the developed and developing worlds and many international organizations such as the IMF, World Bank, and UNCTAD are generally favorable to the idea of international integration (UNCTAD, 1998; UNDP, 1999).

In the public debate, however, globalization is often portrayed as exploitation by the strong (MNCs from rich countries) of the weak (the LDCs). These processes are expected inevitably to lead to social disarray and conflict.[2] Today, most developing countries welcome foreign capital and desire to open up to the international trading system. This is in clear contrast to the 1960s and 1970s when many practiced import substitution policies and formed what seemed to be a solid bloc around the group of 77, which called for a "new international economic order" (NIEO) to replace a biased international capitalist system that was ostensibly exploitative and worked according to a logic of keeping poor countries poor (Krasner, 1985; Bhagwati, 1999; Birdsall and Lawrence, 1999).[3]

The debate on globalization has moved beyond the academic arena. As witnessed by the violent demonstrations in Seattle, Prague, Gothenburg, Genoa, and elsewhere, antiglobalization forces are galvanized into action on the streets. Movements such as ATTAC that are devoted to challenging liberalization of the global economy are spreading. Coalitions against globalization are formed by some unlikely partners. They include supporters of such populist American politicians as Patrick Buchanan and Ross Perot, who want to see an end to US involvement in multilateral treaties and the abolishing of the United Nations system, the World Bank, and the IMF, organized labor interested in protecting domestic markets and jobs, supporters of the Third World devoted to opposing what they see as imperialistic processes behind unfair trade, activists working for a cleaner environment, and anarchists (Micklethwait and Wooldridge, 2000). While anti-globalization activists seem largely to stem from society, galvanizing around diverse communitarian interests, governments of rich nations are also sometimes driven to blame globalization for real and perceived economic failure. The European Commission, for example, blames globalization for unemployment in Europe (Krugman and Venables, 1995). A white paper on globalization issued by the UK government raised concerns about globalization's "human face" (DFID, 2000). Others argue, however, that globalization already benefits the poor. As celebrated economist Jagdish Bhagwati, and others, suggested, Seattle and the noisy protests since have led to the privatization of policymaking where powerful states are trying to balance their domestic concerns with professed commitments to freer trade, rather than firmly committing to open and fair market competition globally (Bhagwati, 1999).

There is a mountain of books on the subject of globalization. Most of the literature is journalistic and anecdotal. The confusion and contentiousness of the issues are captured in popular epithets, which are slung back and forth, such as global-babble, globaloney, and globaldegook. There is much confusion surrounding definitions and terms, making it difficult to evaluate findings and, as a result, to formulate optimal policies. A few scholars have tried to synthesize the debate more systematically, but their voices are hardly heard above the transnational clamor.[4] Given the collapse of the bipolar configuration that dominated the postwar years, the future of global prosperity and peace depend in large measure on the sound and timely management of these processes (Gilpin, 2000). As many argue, a liberal world order requires institutions that stabilize and safeguard international economic cooperation, and form a bulwark against the tendency to retreat, as was the case in the interwar years when countries erected tariff barriers to cushion themselves from postwar economic volatility. This was after all one of the cornerstones of the Bretton Woods system that emerged at the end of World War II and formed the basis of consensus among the Western powers and their allies.

At the end of the Cold War, the developing world is faced with an array of options for development and political change. Improving the prospects of 80 percent of the world's population who live in the developing world on little less than $1 per day (estimated at 1.3 billion people) has replaced the nuclear arms race as the world's most problematic issue (Boutros-Ghali, 1995). Some formerly Third World states are doing remarkably well in terms of raising incomes, instituting good governance, and creating social peace, while others have imploded in violence and disarray, largely due to lack of state capacity and failure to improve the living conditions of people. Many of the failed societies and others teetering on the edge have seen their living standards decrease over the decades. While the term "globalization" is relatively new, the issue of whether or not global structures and agents benefit poor countries, or indeed exploit them, has been at the core of social science research on the problems of development for decades.

Issues of development and underdevelopment were discussed within the framework of modernization and dependency theory, discussions mirrored in the current debate on globalization. While neoliberal, modernization theorists view closer international economic contact as beneficial for poor countries, neo-Marxist, dependency theorists (more frequently called structuralists, or world-system theorists) view such contact as the continuation of neocolonial processes. They appeal to structural theories of imperialism and theories of unequal exchange to argue that international contact between strong and weak states results in adverse socioeconomic outcomes for the poor.[5] They argue in particular that FDI and trade are forms of international capitalist exploitation of developing societies, and that greater contact perpetuates poverty and leads to societal disarray and conflict within the developing world.[6]

In contrast, neoliberal models blame internal processes of bad government and *dirigiste* policies that have shunned global forces as the cause of underdevelopment. They argue that the subversion of domestic and international markets, not their fair functioning, is to blame for underdevelopment. These theories suggest that globalization can prevent narrow interests from dominating the market. The lessening of ideological schisms of the Cold War era and the spread of democracy will improve social welfare, since the created wealth can be redistributed in an accountable, if not consensual, manner. Liberals view the noisy protest that has brought together strange coalitions of groups, particularly within the rich states, as another instance of politically motivated action that protects vested interests, not the truly needy. They advocate that politicians refrain from pandering to vested interests and insist on free market competition, which benefits all.

While I evaluate and test the major theoretical propositions for and against the expected benefits of globalization, I particularly focus on the debates concerning its effects on developing countries. I do not want to discount the debate on globalization's effects on workers in rich countries, a topic that is widely discussed in the literature (Rodrik, 1997; Williamson, 1997; Burtless *et al.*, 1998). But my primary concern is the enormous problem of poverty and the crises of governance in the developing world, problems that are increasingly becoming salient to us all, regardless of where we live. Violent conflict, disease, state collapse, environmental degradation, or uncontrolled human migration—all of these phenomena carry spillovers to everyday life in the farthest corners of the globe. While it does not seem that these problems are located among those states, largely located in East and Southeast Asia, that have practiced open economics, show high trade-to-GDP ratios, and continue to attract much of the World's FDI, the verdict is certainly still out in terms of closer examination of aggregate empirical data as to whether or not and to what extent FDI benefits poor societies.

The most immediate challenge for governments and peoples around the globe will be to distinguish clearly the promises and perils of globalization and formulate the necessary policies that will yield the optimum outcomes. This task will become increasingly difficult given the incoherence of noisy protest, but they are more surmountable today than decades ago when ideology played such a divisive role. Twentieth-century history has been one of unprecedented progress and of massive disruption, but the relatively peaceful end of a decades-long arms race and tense rivalry between the two superpowers suggests the importance of human agency and humanity's capacity for acting constructively in this new century. Indeed, the contours of the 21st century are bound to take shape according to the correlates, and concomitants of globalization.

The advance of globalization

What is globalization and how to assess its consequences are contested issues. As Robert Keohane and Joseph Nye (2000) argued, the importance of faraway places in the history of peoples has ebbed and flowed. Contact between peoples has varied in terms of the degree to which consequential phenomena in social arenas from politics to microbes have affected society (Keohane and Nye, 2000). The current period of economic liberalization is such a flow-phase. I concur with Keohane and Nye's view that the best way to understand waves of globalization is by assessing their "thickness." Europe and China were connected by the silk route plied mainly by bands of traders who transferred such culturally pervasive things as noodles and gunpowder from China to Europe. The present wave of globalization, however, is thicker in that a variety of issues become salient across the globe almost instantaneously, in terms of television pictures and instant communication, and relatively short periods of time are required for the consequences of human migration, financial crises, war, human rights, and environmental issues to be manifested transnationally.

The current wave of globalization is clearly being driven by highly visible and measurable economic processes, such as the growth of trade and the rapid spread of foreign capital (Milner and Keohane, 1996; Bordo *et al.*, 1999). It is also evident in the spread of democratic institutions and adherence to the ideology of the market economy. A newer element of globalization that is still difficult to assess in a balanced way is the emergence of virtual communities through electronic communication. Massive declines in transportation costs and the development of electronic means of communication have shrunk the globe. There is a vast difference between what is possible in the market today (even if it is not fully realized) as opposed to when goods were transferred along the silk route, or when the age of empire globalized economic activity in the 19th century with the advent of the steam engine. Today we live in a truly global age. I first discuss the expansion of economic integration and then the spread of democracy.

When did the present wave of globalization begin? In the political arena, the start of the liberalizing trend has been dated to the mid-1970s (Huntington, 1991). If we look to economic liberalization as a key, we might place the turning point in the late 1970s when far-reaching deregulation began in the US under Jimmy Carter and later reinforced under Ronald Reagan (Henderson, 2000). The UK embraced liberal economic policies after the Thatcher victory in 1979, and subsequently extensive liberalization was introduced in France (from 1982), Australia (from 1983), Canada, and New Zealand (both from 1984). More surprisingly, China started a "rush to capitalism" in 1978, followed by a number of smaller Third World countries and, more significantly, by India in 1991.

For Eastern Europe and the Soviet Union, the fall of the Berlin Wall in 1989 marked a turning point. But changes in world politics had started before that, in what has been referred to as a "quiet cataclysm" (Mueller, 1995). Some heralded the changes as the "end of history" (Fukuyama, 1991). Others have viewed the primary driver of globalization as the "death of distance" (Cairncross, 2001) brought on by the revolution in information and communications technology, also in the late 1970s. Some others interpret what happened during this period as a culture shift that recognized the failure of a modernist project that sought to force-march and force-feed society. Development had to be kinder and gentler to be legitimate, or in fact to be considered as development at all (Sen, 1999). Initially, countries liberalized their internal economies, but in turn this also had consequences for the international economies. Significant steps in this regard were the decision in 1986 to establish a Single Market in the European Union, and the expansion of ASEAN (originally formed in 1967) and the growth of regional groupings such as NAFTA, Mercosur, APEC, and others and the reemergence of GATT and WTO as international instruments for governing the free trade regime. The economic interchange did not simply consist in the movement of goods and money but has also been increasingly accompanied by the movement of labor.

Trade

Rush to capitalism was also a "rush to free trade" (Rodrik, 1998). Integration in the form of trade is not, of course, a new phenomenon. By the end of the 19th century trade exceeded 30 percent of GDP in several European countries. Alberto Alesina and his associates show that for nine European countries with long data series, the average trade-to-GDP ratio was roughly stable until about 1930, when it dropped and stayed down during the depression and war years. After World War II it rose rapidly to the pre-1930 level where it stayed until it started rising again in the early 1970s (Alesina *et al.*, 2000).[7] Of course, during that same period GDP has increased immensely, and the absolute value of trade even more so.

Trade in manufactured and intermediate goods appear to have increased considerably more than trade generally (Bordo *et al.*, 1999). There are also significantly different policymaking environments between the two waves (Baldwin and Martin, 1999). The 19th century's wave of globalization came with imperial, political control of much of the world, so that international trade often meant trade among the powerful states, a handful of actors. At least since the end of World War II, the number of actors on the global trading system has exploded and the political environment of independent, sovereign, national states makes a qualitative difference when trying to assess outcomes of globalization. Moreover, the right comparison of the extent of globalization is perhaps the current situation against perfect integration and not with the 19th century (Frankel, 2000). The movement of goods and capital are still subject to overt and covert barriers, and the free movement of labor is highly restricted. National borders also still matter in other ways. Some studies of the US and Canada, two countries with a long history of free trade, show that despite physical proximity, Americans and Canadians are far more likely to trade within their own borders than across them. Moreover, our own computation of regional averages from 1960 to 1999 shows great unevenness among regions in the share of trade to GDP. Figure 1.1 shows that all regions have increased their share of trade to GDP, but East and Southeast Asia outpace other regions by a wide margin, particularly compared with the low income countries as a group and sub-Saharan Africa (SSA).[8]

Growth of FDI

While trade has been important for a long time, the extent of financial globalization is far wider and deeper today than in the previous wave of globalization in the 19th century. Foreign direct investment now accounts for one-third of global output, three-quarters of commercial technological capacity, and about three-quarters of all world trade (Dunning, 1992). Between 1980 and 1990, FDI quadrupled, increasing at an annual average of 15 percent (UNCTAD, 2000; World Bank, 2001).[9] Between 1983 and

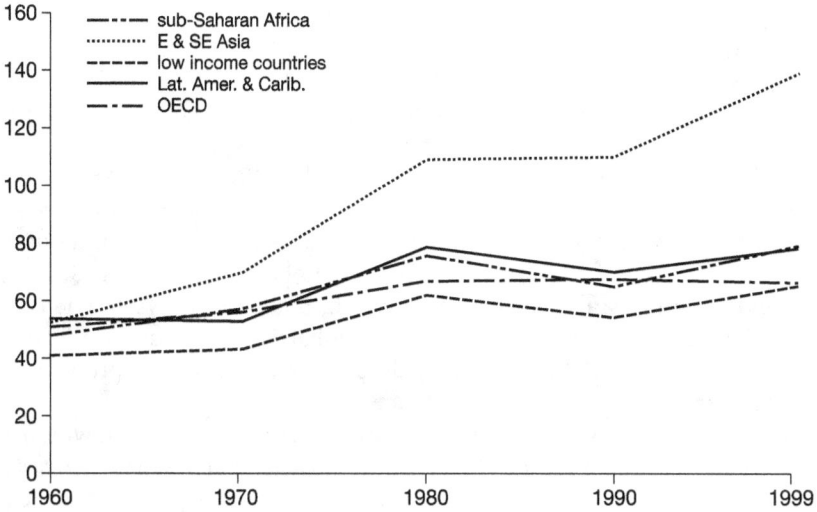

Figure 1.1 Trade-to-GDP ratio by world regions 1960–99. (The data are from the World Bank (2001))

1990, FDI grew at an unprecedented 27 percent per annum, three times faster than the growth of exports and four times that of world output. Indeed, the 1980s has seen what UNCTAD calls "the bulge" in the trend in FDI flows, but the 1980s have been outpaced by the 1990s (UNCTAD, 1994). In 1990, the stock of FDI globally had reached approximately $2,000 billion from a figure a bit under half that. By 1999, a period of just nine years, the stock of FDI more than doubled to reach approximately $4,400 billion (Figure 1.2).

The geographical distribution of FDI remains highly uneven. Between 1985 and 1990, 83 percent of all FDI inflow took place within developed

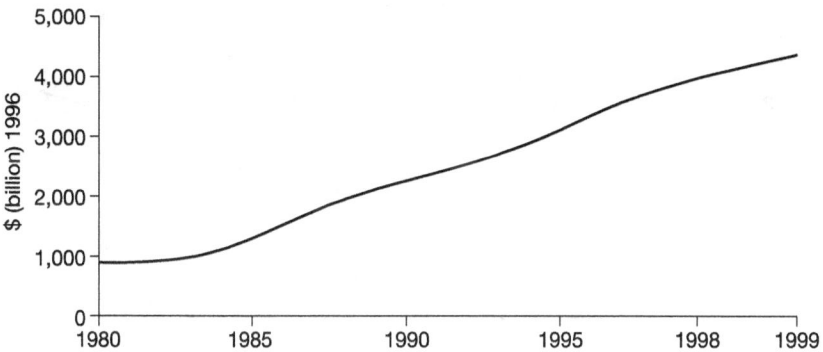

Figure 1.2 Global stock of FDI, 1980–99 (n = 127). (The data are from the UNCTAD (2001))

states. France, Germany, Japan, the US, and the UK accounted for 56 percent of worldwide inflow between 1980 and 1990 (UNCTAD, 1994). In 1960, 48 percent of all FDI originated from the US. In 1990, the US share of FDI around the globe had shrunk to 26 percent, with Japan becoming a major capital exporter. In 1990, approximately 79 percent of the total inward FDI stock globally could be found within 20 developed states. By 1999, this figure was down to 69 percent with China accounting for almost 7 percent of global stock by itself. All of Africa, with its abundant natural resources, accounts for a mere 2 percent of global stock. With regard to FDI, globalization still has a long way to go, and there is even some evidence that certain areas are becoming less globalized in terms of trade and investment ratios to GDP.[10] For many developing countries, the problem is how to attract FDI, not how to repel it.

Recent trends show, however, that more investment is now flowing to poorer countries. Between 1980 and 1990, the mean annual rate of investment for LDCs was 8 percent, which increased to 12.4 percent between 1990 and 1997. Moreover, the FDI stock-to-GDP ratio (a standard measure of the internationalization of the economy) increased from 8 percent in 1980 to 14 percent by 1990 and 25 percent in 1997 (Figure 1.3). The correlation between the level of trade to GDP and the FDI stock-to-GDP ratio increased from 0.47 for 1980 to 0.58 for 1990 and 0.62 for 1997. Higher levels of international capital seem to be tied to increasing levels of international trade within economies. Some studies suggest that FDI is responsible for driving greater levels of trade but that initially more open economies also seemed to have attracted greater amounts of FDI (de Melo, 1999).

For a sample of 20 rich countries (the main capital exporters), the average FDI stock-to-GDP ratio was 8 percent in 1980, 13 percent in 1990, and 22 percent in 1998 respectively. Clearly, both poorer countries and the richest ones are becoming internationalized at a rather rapid rate according to the FDI stock-to-GDP ratio (see Figure 1.3).

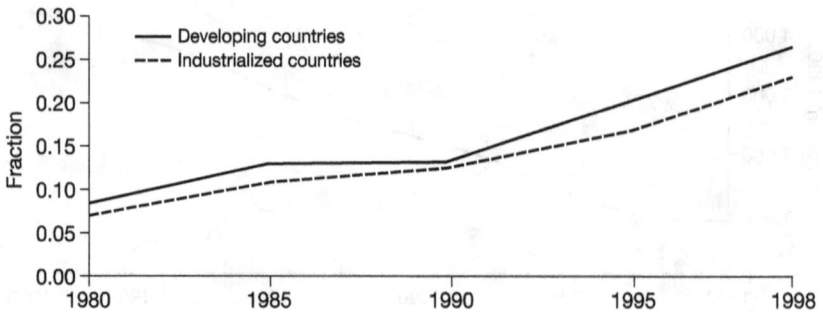

Figure 1.3 FDI stock-to-GDP ratio in industrialized and developing countries. Y-axis represents fraction of FDI stock to GDP.

The level of internationalization is now almost equal in rich and poor countries.[11] FDI in the rich countries is clearly driven by technological and market factors. For the poor countries, much of this is owed to drastic change in attitude of governments towards FDI, a major impediment in the past.

Growth of democracy

By democracy I broadly mean governance by the people. There are numerous suggestions for how to define it more precisely, and for how to measure it. One widely accepted notion of modern, liberal democracy is Robert Dahl's concept of polyarchy (Dahl, 1971). Polyarchy is the product of *political competition* and *political participation*. This is closely in line with a measure of democracy developed by Tatu Vanhanen (Vanhanen, 2000). I examine the relevance of identifying qualitative aspects based on these dimensions of democracy, particularly in relation to economic growth, in later chapters. The Polity index, another frequently cited measure, conceptualizes democracy largely in institutional terms, with particular emphasis on *restraints on executive power*, but this measure is largely subjectively derived. A third approach starts from *civil and political rights*, which incorporate factors relating to civil liberties and human rights, also subjectively derived (Freedom House, 2002).[12]

Democratic government has spread over time, but not in a linear fashion. Samuel Huntington identifies three broad waves of democratization, which have been verified in quantitative studies (Huntington, 1991). The first wave peaked after World War I and was followed by a period when the two totalitarian movements that arose in Europe reversed democracy in their home countries as well as in many of their neighbors. After the fall of fascism in 1945 followed soon by decolonization, democracy was once again on an upward trend, as illustrated in Figure 1.4.[13]

The second wave of democratization was soon reversed, however, with the continued growth of communism and the failure of many postcolonial democracies to take hold. Not until the mid-1970s did the third wave begin, initially with the decline of military rule in Southern Europe and then powerfully reinforced after the fall of communism in 1989. The third wave is still continuing, and has brought the world to a point where more countries and a higher proportion of its peoples live under democratic rule than ever before. Although there have been reversals in some countries and pessimistic voices about the end of the third wave have been raised from time to time, the trend continues to point upwards.

As demonstrated by Figure 1.4, the third wave of democratization largely coincides in time with the period identified as the boom period of globalization. Only a little over a decade ago, many prognosticated the limits of democratization because of what they saw to be the growth of "bureaucratic authoritarianism" with the advance of modernization in the

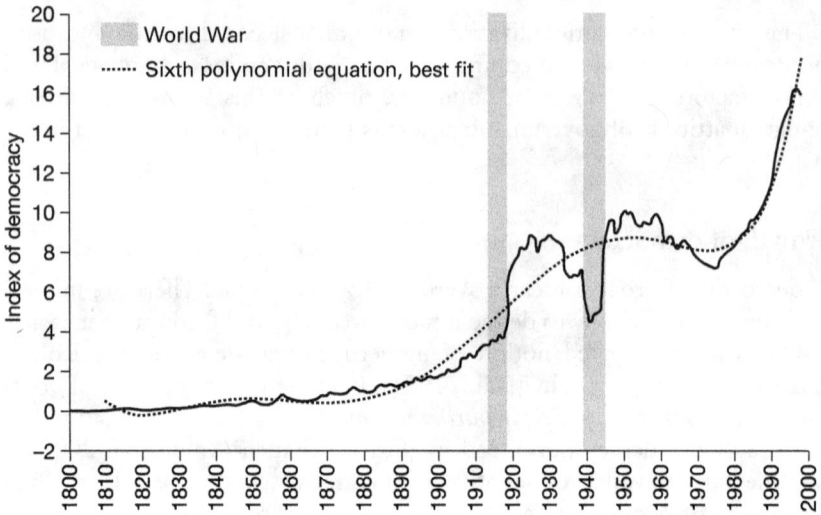

Figure 1.4 The growth of democracy 1800–2000. (This figure shows the annual
value of the democracy measure created by Vanhanen (2000) and a
trend line based on the sixth polynomial created from data available
at www.prio.no/jpr/datasets.asp)

developing world (O'Donnell, 1973). Dependency theorists in particular
would not have been able to predict such transformation under liberal economic conditions of increased trade and investment. We may not have
reached the "end of history" because movement in reverse has been the historical pattern, but the transformation is remarkable. There is no denying
what many herald as the hallmarks of our age, economic and political liberalization. The question is, what might we expect in terms of future trends
in development?

Growth of income and welfare

One standard measure of the rate of development is the rate of increase of
the level of per capita income, or economic growth. Standard neoclassical
theory predicts that poorer countries grow faster on average than richer
countries because of diminishing returns to capital, usually called the
Solow model after the Nobel prizewinning economist. Poor countries were
expected to converge with the rich over time because of their higher capacity for absorbing capital. Convergence, however, failed by and large to
occur. As Figure 1.5 shows, the poor countries' average growth collapsed
in the 1980s compared to the rich countries, hence there was divergence of
income, not convergence.

Contrarily, the East Asian Tigers have maintained a high level of growth
on average, which has been declining since the 1980s, but the graphic illustrates the gaps in performance between the rich and poor countries and the

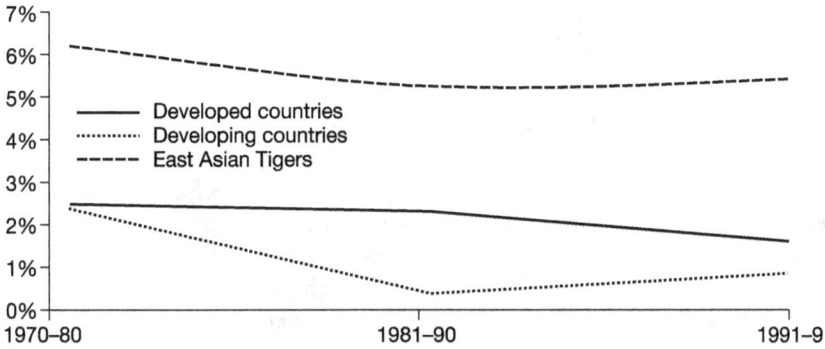

Figure 1.5 Period average economic growth rates, 1970–80, 1981–90, 1991–9. (The growth rates are computed with per capital income data from Easterly and Sewadeh (2001) using the World Bank's least-squares method. See Data appendix for details.)

East Asian NICs which are playing catch-up with the rich. New growth theories have discarded the notion of diminishing returns to capital, showing instead increasing returns to human capital (technology and ideas), which explains why the rich do not always slow down and why some poor countries have failed to grow at all. Poorer countries with higher initial endowments of human capital grew faster than the rich countries in the postwar years (Barro, 1991; Temple, 1999). East and Southeast Asia's spectacular growth performance in the postwar years is explained as being driven to a large extent by that region's higher levels of human capital. In Africa, on the other hand, the recent growth record is dismal, with a few striking exceptions (Botswana, Mauritius).

There are many objections to GDP per capita as a measure of welfare: wealth can be unevenly distributed (even to the point where a growing average is accompanied by increasing impoverishment); it can be created at the cost of pollution, hazardous work, etc. The UN provides several alternative indices of welfare, such as the Human Development Index (a composite measure of life expectancy, education, and material standard of living) and the Rate of Progress, which measures the rate of reduction of under-five mortality (UNICEF, 2000). While it is often argued that economic growth and human welfare do not work in tandem, the weight of the evidence suggests that they most certainly do (Lal and Myint, 1996; Chen and Ravallion, 1998; Dollar and Kraay, 2000).

Of course, growth alone is not enough as UNICEF (2000) claims, because there is a role for policy. Increasing income and taxable wealth, however, allow governments to implement the right policies for achieving other objectives. Clearly, some countries fail to insure progress on indicators such as health and education despite growth, and well-targeted policy that improves health and education will contribute to growth, but even well-meaning policymakers must create the conditions that allow them the financial means for achieving ends beyond growth. A plethora of recent studies find that economic growth is strongly related to human welfare, defined in terms of socioenvironmental dimensions, such as longevity and education, access to basic needs, and the reduction of the inequality of income (Lal and Myint, 1996; Deininger and Squire, 1997; Chen and Ravallion, 1998; Dollar and Kraay, 2000). One study concludes that "the developing countries suffering from low growth . . . are generally worse off with respect to macro-economic stability and redistributive justice as compared to those enjoying medium growth to high growth" (Naqvi, 1996).

Human welfare can also be measured in terms of consumption of goods weighed against the time spent on acquiring them. Such a comparison is particularly valid for gauging the quality of life of today's poor, who aspire to consume more than they are able to. Bradford DeLong provided an interesting discussion on this score (DeLong, 2000). The material standard of living and human productive capability have exploded in the 20th century. For example, what took a worker in 1890 an hour's worth of labor to produce on average can be done today in seven minutes. DeLong looked at the prices of various commodities in a Montgomery Ward Catalogue and compared them with hourly wages so that the relative time spent acquiring a good can be compared over time. A bicycle would have cost 260 hours of work in 1895 for an average working person compared to 7.2 hours in 2000—1/36th as much in labor time. A six-volume set of books by Horatio Alger cost 1/34th the labor time, a 100-piece dinner set cost 1/12th the labor time, etc. Only silverware will cost more today, but given the availability of stainless steel, this is hardly a necessary commodity—a teaspoon made of stainless steel would be 1/50th the cost in labor time! Much of DeLong's analysis was based on data from the United States, but the analysis surely holds for many developing countries that are part of "the world that trade has created" since at least the 1400s (Pomeranz and Topik, 1998).

In the case against globalization, inequality—alleged to be rising—plays a central role. And, indeed, the gap in income and other forms of welfare between rich and poor citizens of the world is enormous. This is true whether one thinks in terms of disparities in consumption, human development indicators such as literacy and health, or risks to life and limb from natural and man-made catastrophes, such as war, famine, and everyday violence. Globally, 20 percent of the world's population, all of whom hail from the rich states, account for a full 86 percent of total private consumption expenditures, with the poorest 20 percent accounting for a minuscule 1.3 percent (UNDP, 1998). The richest country had 115 times the per capita income of the poorest. It is frequently argued that the gap between rich and poor states has been growing in the postwar years, with only a handful of middle-income countries closing the gap with the leaders. "Inequality between countries has . . . increased," argues the *Human Development Report 1999* (UNDP, 1999). Most countries that were poor in the 1950s and 1960s remain poor today, and the majority of people in the least developed countries consume less than they did 25 years ago. The era of high growth, which followed the end of World War II has benefited only a select group of countries (Gilpin, 1987; Maddison, 1989; Spero, 1990; Olson, 1996).

Closing the ever-diverging gap between the rich and poor countries has rapidly become a high priority, not least because of growing radicalism that violently targets rich countries directly through acts of mass terror, exemplified by the attacks on the World Trade Center, Twin Towers, in New York. Such acts of terror are alleged to be carried out by radicals outraged at global disparities between rich and poor, aimed at an unfair, inequitable world system dominated by the power and interests of the West, particularly of the United States.

Even if the real motives of groups like al-Qaeda are not based on the reality of this disparity, the popularity of such movements is driven by the power of this stark reality. Therefore, greater divergence can only be stymied by accelerated growth in poor countries. Spurring investment, particularly private investment, and thereby economic growth is going to be the major source of poverty alleviation given that foreign aid budgets have reached their lowest levels in history. The end of the Cold War has facilitated the sharp reduction in foreign aid budgets, now a mere 0.25 percent of the GNP on average of the donor countries, and the decline will most likely continue (UNDP, 1998). The great irony is that just when aid could have been used effectively given the removal of geopolitical imperatives that led to massive misallocation of aid in the past, foreign aid budgets have shrunk to nothing today.

The view that inequality within countries has been increasing during the period of globalization is contested. Comparisons on the basis of income measures adjusted for purchasing power (PPP) indicate that inequality seems to have been decreasing over the period 1965–97 when using a measure that takes account of the entire range of the income distribution (the Gini index). Studies using income data that are not adjusted for price differences, generally report rising income inequality. For studies using more limited parts of the income distribution, the results depend on what comparisons are made. Comparing the richest and poorest 20 percent, some report lower inequality (Melchior *et al.*, 2000). Reports of higher inequality are usually based either on figures not adjusted for price differences or on more limited parts of the income distribution (highest/lowest 10 percent or even highest/lowest country). Prior to 1960, world income inequality seems to have been increasing. The more recent decline is consistent with the inverted U-curve posited by Simon Kuznets (Kuznets, 1966). Given that so many developing countries are struggling to come out of stagnation and poverty, we should expect many of them to be on the upturn of the Kuznets curve, but we may very well expect downward trends with rising income and increasing levels of democracy (Barro, 1998). Robert

Barro confirmed the Kuznets curve on recent data, and O' Rourke (2001) argued that the growth of inequality in the past 200 years may be attributed to between-country inequality, and that the recent trend shows convergence.

While there is compelling evidence to show that between-country inequality in particular has been rising in the postwar years, particularly between 1980 and 1999, much of the increase in the Gini index may be attributed to the failure of growth in much of Africa and Latin America and the collapse of the middle class in the former Soviet Bloc (Milanovic, 2001). If, however, the sample is weighted by global population, rather than nation state, there is a net decline in inequality, largely driven by the rapid growth of Chinese income, which has quadrupled in comparison with mean world income. Moreover, urban China's rapid growth relative to rural China and India and the steady growth rate of the industrialized countries in Western Europe and North America account for much of the inequality in global terms. The findings of this thorough study, which uses household surveys and PPP-based GDPs to measure world income, underwrite the importance of generating growth where it has failed. As I outline below, trade and investment will be key in generating badly needed growth, and good macropolicies will also contribute towards achieving social peace, which is threatened by absolute poverty. Eliminating poverty—now a key element of the policy of the World Bank and other international agencies—might well be given priority over the reduction of inequality per se.

Open markets and development

Classical observers recognized the benefits of mutual gain from trade and exchange. John Stuart Mill observed that "the opening of foreign trade . . . sometimes works a sort of industrial revolution in a country whose resources were previously underdeveloped" (Todaro, 1977). With the flow of goods, capital, and technology, LDCs are expected to gain through an open market. The example of enormous gains made by the miracle economies of East and Southeast Asia that practiced export-led growth strategies are often contrasted with the failure of the import-substitution strategies that were followed by many other states, notably those in Latin America, Africa, and South Asia (Gilpin, 1987). As one scholar put it, "trade, trade, and more trade was what propelled the Pacific-rim states out of agrarian destitution or post-World War II destruction and decline into world economic prominence" (Aikman, 1986). Foreign capital and trade played a crucial role in developing the technological capabilities of the East Asian NICS, such as Taiwan and South Korea (Kuznets, 1966; Amsden, 1988).

New evidence challenges the view held by structural theorists that foreign capital and trade worked against the poor countries. Theoretically, neoliberals have long argued that there are substantial benefits from foreign capital for creating economic development. According to standard neoclassical theories economic growth is based on the utilization of land, labor, and capital in the productive process. Since developing nations in general have underutilized land and labor and exhibit low savings rates, the marginal productivity of capital is likely to be greater in these areas. Thus, neoliberal theories of development assume that interdependence between the developed and the developing countries would serve to benefit the latter because capital will flow from rich to poor areas where the returns on capital investments would be highest, helping to bring about a transformation of "backward" societies. Therefore, capital-poor developing states should benefit from the expected infusion of capital from the capital-rich, industrialized states. Moreover, neoliberals place particular emphasis on FDI to act as an engine of growth through the transfer of technology. Simon Kuznets linked the productivity of the industrialized, Western states to the extended application of science and technology to the problems of production. According to Kuznets, the basis of modern society is inextricably linked to the application of advanced technologies, and the economic prospects of developing states depend mostly on the transfer of transnational knowledge and technology from rich to poor states.

In this sense, investment by MNCs from the richer states is a basic mechanism for the transfer of technology from those that have it to those that do not. Poor states are not merely capital depositories; they also benefit from the technologies embodied in the capital invested from abroad, and especially in the case of FDI as opposed to other forms of capital transfers from rich to poor states. Since developing countries lack the managerial and technical skills required for fueling development, foreign direct investment in particular has been seen as a key element in North–South interaction that aided the process of economic growth and the convergence of incomes between rich and poor. Through this process of the diffusion of capital and technology, developing countries were expected to take off into self-sustaining growth, achieving higher stages of development and catching up with the rich (Rostow, 1960). Not only does FDI bring technology, but the MNC also transfers a package of institutional attributes of the modern corporation that helps to transform tradition-bound, particularistic societies of the developing areas. Indeed, some recent studies conclude that FDI has been one of the most effective means for the transfer of technology and of knowledge (Dunning and Hamdani, 1997). These studies have concluded that multinational capital is crucial for improving productivity and standards of living in developing areas.

Neoliberals also argue the importance of open markets for economic development. According to them, LDCs benefit from such an arrangement because states with small markets, as is the case with most LDCs, gain access to the much larger markets of the industrialized areas. This process allows small states to exploit economies of scale. Moreover, trade is expected to diffuse knowledge because it encourages learning by doing. The growth of the productive capacity of an economy is best realized through continued specialization and exposure to the global marketplace.[14] The recent evidence on openness and rapid economic growth is less ambiguous than the findings on FDI. According to one widely cited study that estimates the robustness of a multitude of variables thought to influence growth, trade to GDP (openness) was one of two variables exhibiting a robust relationship to growth, working through investment (Levine and Renelt, 1992). Recent findings are even less ambiguous about the effects of trade on income (Baldwin and Seghezza, 1996) and on the growth of income of the poor in particular (Dollar and Kraay, 2000). My focus throughout the rest of this book will be on FDI, which is the more contentious issue among those who are vehemently opposed to the idea of globalization. These theories are far less apparent in economics but have come to dominate the other social sciences, particularly sociology and political science. I address these concerns next.

2 Globalization and development

Theory old and new

Introduction

This chapter explores the theoretical divisions between the liberal perspective and the neo-Marxist, dependency and world-systems perspectives on foreign capital and economic development. By and large, these two perspectives dominated the development debates of the past two decades, and strong echoes of these debates reverberate in the new debates between the optimists and pessimists on the future of globalization. This chapter explores the theoretical debates on both positions on the effects of foreign capital on economic growth, considering especially recent controversies that form the bases of the empirical analyses of the present study presented in Chapter 3. First, however, I trace the bases of the new arguments and link them to older theory.

The ideological barriers to North–South cooperation notwithstanding, the collapse of the East–West dimension of world politics offers reasons to be optimistic. There has been a dilution of nationalist and ideologically motivated economic policies in much of the developing world. In fact, there is an argument to be made that the pragmatism of much of the South may have much to do with the newfound pragmatism among the former socialist-communist states. The rise of the East Asian NICs from colonial status to economic power coupled with the success of many other states in Southeast Asia signaled the benefits of outward orientation, particularly export-led growth over import-substitution industrialization (ISI) (Waterbury, 1999). Today, many states are following more "orthodox" and "rational" paths to economic policymaking, given the apparent failure of ISI (Maddison, 1989). The new policy mode is generally referred to as the "Washington Consensus," a large part of which is the call to finance development with FDI and liberalization of trade (Williamson, 1994).

The change from ideology to pragmatism was echoed early by the architect of China's successful market-based reforms, Deng Xiaoping, who made such statements as "no country can now develop by closing its doors . . . Isolation landed China in poverty, backwardness, and ignorance" and "I don't care if the cat is white or black as long as it catches mice" (quoted in Gilpin, 1987: 294). The Vietnamese foreign minister, Nguyen Co Thach, justified his country's reforms thus: "The path of autarky and closed-door policy is the path to backwardness and poverty. To cope with the challenges of history, the only path for us is to associate the Vietnamese economy with the world economy" (Nhandan, 1989). More recently, other notable ideologues against capitalist principles have joined the chorus. The Cuban president, Fidel Castro, now seeks to "rectify" the path to socialism by hailing the virtues of foreign capital and foreign trade. According to one of his speeches:

> It is not that we thought that foreign investment was absolutely inconceivable. I think that within the tenets of socialism, even trying to build the most perfect socialism possible, there can be merits in foreign investment, where the foreign entrepreneur provides the capital, the technology and the markets, or any part of these three aspects.
>
> (Quoted in Cross, 1995: 258)

The end of ideologically motivated intransigence, the acknowledgment of the failures of irrational, *dirigiste* policies, coupled with the third wave of democracy, led to the belief that greater cooperation among states is possible for determining what is becoming an increasingly common global future (World Bank, 1992). The extent of these changes is borne out by the successful conclusion of the Uruguay round of the General Agreement on Trade and Tariffs (the GATT) and the establishment of a World Trade Organization (WTO). These institutions are still far from perfect and are controversial, but despite the disagreements among the various members of these organizations, they are expected to act as efficient conduits for cooperatively addressing North–South concerns about trade, aid, and development. According to some, the economic adjustments undertaken by many states to restructure their economies toward more market-friendly directions will yield enormous gain in coming decades (World Bank, 1992; Salamon, 1994).[1] We may have witnessed an end to open "structural conflict" between North and South that characterized much of global economic relations after the oil shocks of the 1970s (Krasner, 1985). Such optimism notwithstanding, opponents of liberalization are also winning battles. For example, a broad coalition of activists came together to scuttle the MAI on the basis that MNCs exploit LDCs and that the MAI would institutionalize such exploitation (Graham, 2000).

Despite the debates on the streets, largely among activists based in the West, the end of nonmarket ideology in the South has improved conditions for generating growth. Ideology alone does not cause growth, however, and the reality is that much of the poor world remains mired in poverty and resultant social problems associated with stagnant growth. Most countries remain constrained by the lack of capital. The tightening of the international capital markets, resulting mainly from the huge budget deficits that are maintained by some of the industrialized nations, heavy indebted-ness, bad creditworthiness of many of the LDCs, which have been forced to default on their debt, and the demand for capital by the former communist countries now joining the global market, do not bode well for most poor developing countries (Spero, 1990). Without investment, there cannot be growth, and without sufficient growth, there is little possibility for enhanc-ing the welfare and the living standards of the world's poor (Naqvi, 1996). Moreover, many of the LDCs, who are highly dependent on primary commodity exports, the prices of which fluctuate wildly, lack the entre-preneurial, managerial, and technological know-how to diversify their economies in an increasingly competitive global environment.

Such realities on the ground have led to arguments suggesting that FDI has an important role to play. FDI is supposed to offset debt–equity imbal-ances, assist structural adjustment through production and marketing of exports and competitive import substitutes, and transfer state-of-the-art technologies (United Nations, 1988; Ahiakpor, 1990; Lele and Nabi, 1991; United Nations, 1992; United Nations, 1995; World Bank, 1995; World Bank, 1996a; Dunning and Hamdani, 1997). The multinational corpora-tion, it has been argued, will be a source of finance and know-how, creating much-needed jobs. The United Nations recognized FDI as a potential "engine of growth" in one of its publications devoted to multinational cor-porations (United Nations, 1992). The optimism is greatly buoyed by the fact that, finally, liberal economic policies and liberal politics can function unimpeded without having to contend with the polarized politics of the Cold War. Stability as a result of democracy and good government will also bring capital and economic growth in its wake, closing the positive feed-back loop created by foreign capital and good government. Apparently, "all good things" are expected to "go together."

The liberal view is challenged, however, by a plethora of views in recent scholarly books and journal articles. The critics of the liberal view range from the ultraright to the ultraleft with many groups in between. For the rightist and ultranationalists, globalization is an attack on sovereignty, but this view prevails predominantly among groups within the industrialized states. These groups may also engage in the politics of identity where glob-alization is equated with increased immigration. In terms of globalization's effects on the South, however, the critics tend to be left-oriented. These observers argue that the current changes are a harbinger of the intensifica-tion of "imperialist" control of the powerless poor by the powerful rich. Mixed in with concerns for the poor in the developing world is a concern for the global environment, which is apparently under threat by the onslaught of capitalist greed and ill-conceived liberalization (Brecher and Costello, 1994; Rich, 1995).

The pessimists counter liberal arguments by suggesting that the condi-tions being imposed on weaker states by those who control capital are exploitative. They argue that since the lines between what is domestic and what is international are becoming increasingly blurred, the poor will be left defenseless, individuals and groups not conforming to the logic of globalization will have no champions, and democracy itself will be stunted.[2] In other words, while state and individual sovereignty decrease, it is argued that "global capital" will be master (Gill, 1995; Korten, 2001). Even the spread of democracy and the emphasis on the rule of law are seen to be processes by which the powerful countries and corporations "make the world safe" for private and transnational capital at the expense of real development (Willett, 2001). The following is representative of this line of argumentation: "This growing transnationalism has also led to the concentration of economic power in the hands of giant multinational corporations where most strategic decisions are made. The natural consequence of these developments has been the deepening of inequalities . . . and increasing peripheralization of developing countries" (Eder, 1994: 65).

What's more, these observers argue that democratic decisionmaking could be under threat given that foreign capital is in a position to impose its will on the governments of poor countries (Korany, 1994; Gill, 1995; Armijo, 1999a).

The new debate on globalization is reminiscent of the earlier debates between the neoliberal theories of development and the "structuralist" (dependency) theories that have dominated development studies in the past three decades.[3] Among the pessimists in the LDCs, Samir Amin (1990) and others continue to argue that global integration can only cause the "maldevelopment" of developing countries. Those who followed an autarkic path to development, or socialism, were victims of international capitalist machinations, driven largely by the security interests of the powerful North American and Western European states, MNCs, and banks, and their collapse had nothing to do with their own weight (Gills and Qadir, 1995). They argue that the best option for developing countries is to "delink" from the international capitalist system. In the current debate on global integration, however, the pessimistic views are not just those of third-world ideologues and philosophers.

As some observers claim, it is one of the "paradoxes of our modern age" that Americans (and Western Europeans), who have for so long been the champions of economic integration and free market economics, are increasingly raising doubts about the processes driving globalization, particularly the spread of FDI and trade (Burtless *et al.*, 1998: ix). The pessimistic trend was evident early in the debates over the North American Free Trade Agreement (NAFTA) and the fast-track trade negotiations in the United States Congress. Recent opinion surveys of Americans show that 50 percent of those polled thought that globalization would cause more harm than good (Burtless *et al.*, 1998: 6). While the signs were there, it was not until the 1999 World Trade Organization summit in Seattle that the breadth and depth of antiglobalization feeling were displayed. Ever since, all kinds of problems have been connected to economic liberalization and globalization.

The discussion above has been a mere sampling of the contentiousness of the issue of globalization as it plays out in the popular media, politics, and academia. As some suggest quite presciently, the rancorous debate within academia cautions optimism about the future of global cooperation on the "ground floor of life" (von Laue, 1987). Objective analyses and testing of these theories and propositions are not merely "academic," but objectively derived empirical evidence will serve to enhance our understanding of global and transnational phenomena more clearly for making crucial policy. Rigorous testing of the propositions about the effects of the two most salient pillars of globalization—foreign capital and democracy—with clearly articulated hypotheses that are theoretically relevant, will provide systematic understanding of the complex, evolving phenomenon of globalization. This is especially warranted now given that policymakers around the globe are groping for answers to the complex questions that globalization raises.

The neoliberals and development

Neoliberals argue that there are substantial benefits of foreign capital for creating economic development. According to the standard neoclassical theories, economic growth occurs with the utilization of land, labor, and capital in the productive process. These growth models predict that the more the labor, the more the land; or the more the capital, the faster the growth. Since developing nations in general have underutilized land and labor and exhibit low savings rates, the marginal productivity of capital is supposed to be greater in these areas. Thus, neoclassical growth theory has viewed that open-capital flows between the developed and the developing countries would serve to benefit the latter because capital will flow from rich to poor areas where the returns to capital investments would be highest. Capital-poor developing states should be the beneficiaries of the expected infusion of capital from the capital-rich, industrialized states (I examine this question in greater detail below).

Moreover, neoliberals are apt to place particular emphasis on the benefits of FDI as an "engine of growth." This reasoning stems from the orthodox belief that capital accumulation, human capital augmentation, and the transfer of technology are the hallmarks of development. Simon Kuznets linked the productivity of the industrialized, Western states purely to the extended application of science and technology to the problems of production (Kuznets, 1966). According to Kuznets, the basis of modern society is inextricably linked to the application of advanced technologies, and the economic prospects of developing states depend mostly on the transfer of transnational knowledge and technology from rich to poor states.

In this sense, investments of MNCs from the richer states are ostensibly one basic mechanism for the transfer of technology from those who have it to those who do not. Poor states are not merely capital depositories, but they also benefit from the technologies embodied in the capital invested from abroad, and especially in the case of foreign direct investment as opposed to other forms of capital transfers from rich to poor states. Since developing countries lack the managerial and technical skills required for generating industrialization, foreign direct investment in particular was thought to be a key element of North–South interaction that aided the process of economic growth and the convergence of incomes between rich and poor. Through this process of the diffusion of capital and technology, developing countries were expected to "take off" into self-sustaining growth, achieving higher stages of development and "catching up" with the rich (Rostow, 1960).

Within this theoretical framework, the MNC is a vehicle for capital and technology transfer from the developed to the developing world. The tacit assumption underlying this perspective is that the developing world is "underdeveloped" because of institutional and cultural barriers to modernization, which have to give way to new organizational principles brought from afar. Thus, MNCs become major instruments of modernization by locating their activities in less developed areas. Not only do they bring capital and technology, but they also provide a package of "institutional" attributes of the modern corporation that would transfer ultimately to the tradition-bound, particularistic societies of the developing areas. The MNC also provides the institutional tools, or organizational principles, that remove barriers to productivity. Indeed, some recent studies (Dunning and Hamdani, 1997) conclude that FDI has been one of the most effective means for the transfer of technology and of knowledge. These studies have concluded that multinational capital is crucial for improving productivity and standards of living in developing areas.

Neoliberals also argue the importance of open markets for economic development. According to them, LDCs benefit from such an arrangement because states with small markets, as is the case with most LDCs, gain access to the much larger markets of the industrialized areas. This process allows small states to exploit economies of scale. Moreover, trade is expected to diffuse knowledge because it encourages "learning by doing" (Arrow, 1962). For neoliberals, the growth and development of LDCs hinge crucially on the issue of trade and investment. Since the "stuff" of development is the growth of the productive capacity of an economy, these theorists believe that "efficiency" is best realized through continued specialization and exposure to the global marketplace.[4]

John Stuart Mill was an early observer who wrote that "the opening of foreign trade . . . sometimes works a sort of industrial revolution in a country whose resources were previously underdeveloped" (quoted in Todaro, 1977: 33). With the flow of goods, capital, and technology, LDCs are expected to gain through an open market. The example of enormous gains made by the "miracle" economies of East and Southeast Asia that practiced "export-led" growth strategies are often contrasted with the failure of the "import-substitution" strategies that were followed by many other states, notably those in Latin America, Africa, and South Asia (Gilpin, 1987). In general, liberal theories favor an interdependent world economy where specialization, free trade, and the division of labor enhance the prospects of absolute gain by all participants, even if the trajectories of development among states will be uneven. For liberals, free trade and investment is not a zero-sum game where someone loses and others gain, but a process of creative destruction that comes with progress, which has to be managed and kept within bounds.

Liberal theories of economic development, however, recognize that an interdependent world, working on the basis of free markets and linkages to the global economy, does not necessarily promote development evenly. Indeed, it is expected that poorer states may gain at rates faster than the relatively rich because of "advantages of backwardness" (Gerschenkron, 1962). Just like Kuznets's (1966) prediction about inequality within states, the widening inequality with the advent of industrialization between states leads to the slowing down of the rich and the gradual catch up of the poor following a similar path. The entire process of development generally follows the logic of competition and advancement, where development is dependent upon the adaptation of societies to the exigencies of market competition. Backwardness is advantageous in this process because diffusion takes place from the "core" industrialized countries to the peripheries at faster rates than the core is able to adopt what Simon Kuznets (1966: 5) termed "epochal" innovations in leading sectors. This process in operation is what some argue leads to the "rise and decline" of states (Gilpin, 1981; Olson, 1982), and it is the "law of uneven development" that V. I. Lenin proposed was a permanent feature of capitalism.

In time, it became apparent that the diffusion of capital and technology from rich to poor did not happen to the extent and degree that neoclassical theories of economic development had predicted in the wake of postwar enthusiasm for development. Capital did not run rampant in developing countries. In fact, developing countries, which were freshly independent, developed biased policies towards multinationals. As Paul Romer has commented, "One of the legacies of colonialism is an aversion in some developing countries to any contact or exchange with firms from industrial economies. Interaction with multinational firms is sometimes permitted, but only on terms that are so restrictive and unattractive that few foreign firms decide to participate" (Romer, 1993: 547).

The pattern of FDI flows into the poor areas of the world in the past three decades is illustrative of the general problem. While FDI has surpassed bank lending and portfolio capital as the major source of capital for poor countries, its spread within the developing world is uneven (IMF, 2000). As Figure 2.1 illustrates, of the share of FDI that is located in poor countries, the regional shares are unevenly distributed.

A handful of countries in East and Southeast Asia have over 50 percent

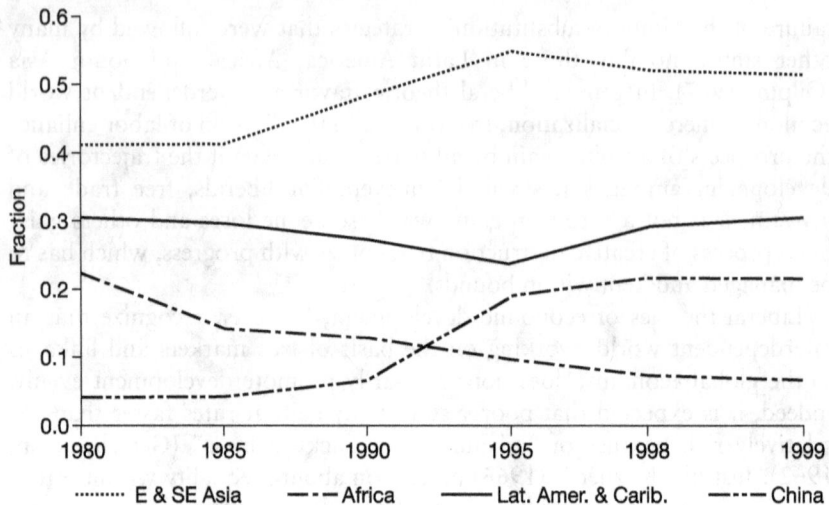

Figure 2.1 Regional shares of FDI stock in total LDC stock

of the total LDC stock with China containing more than 20 percent of the share of LDC stock. Africa's share of FDI has been steadily declining and stands at just under 10 percent of LDC stock. Thus, most of Africa, South Asia, and Latin America have been bypassed.[5] The evidence suggests that foreign capital does not "run rampant" among the poor countries in the world as many pessimists on globalization seem to suggest.

Capital-poor developing states are locked in competition for a better share of FDI flows. This is especially hard as the industrialized states are also vying fiercely to attract foreign capital for fueling their growth. There is still no theory on the determinants of FDI, but rather, various approaches and general trends have been identified. To compound the problem, much of the work undertaken so far has been by economists, who have, by and large, concentrated on economic factors as determinants. On the other hand, sociologists and political scientists have variously applied political and social factors for determining FDI, many of these studies concentrating on the developing countries, where the issue of political stability was naturally a major concern (Schneider and Frey, 1985). Recent research in new growth theory has begun to factor in "human capital" as a major determinant of FDI (Lucas, 1990). As many studies have concluded, however, it has been the attitudes of governments in the developing world towards FDI that has been a major determinant of FDI flows there (United Nations, 1991; Amirahmadi and Wu, 1994).

Various formalized theories of the multinational corporation also attempt to explain the growth of FDI.[6] According to some it is the imperfections in markets that promote transfers of capital to areas that offer higher returns (Kindleberger, 1975). As the theory suggests, MNC activities are hampered by the lack of perfect information, hence MNCs are forced to venture abroad to safeguard their profits within existing markets. Thus, according to Kindleberger (1975: 61), "in a world of perfect competition for goods and factors, direct investment cannot exist." Raymond Vernon (1971) suggested that growth of FDI is caused by the oligopolistic nature of the MNC as an organization. The growth of FDI is a function of the institutional necessity for an MNC to gather as much market share as possible because of temporary technological advantages (Vernon, 1971). Thus, it is the "product cycle" that determines why firms venture abroad.

Stephen Hymer (1972) offered a slight variant of this theory. He argued that, while it is the "product cycle" that drives FDI, firms locate in other markets because it is cheaper to seek oligopolistic rents with an aging product. The MNC merely markets an aging product elsewhere, such as in the developing areas, where this product would still be relatively competitive, rather than developing a new product in the existing market. In this way, oligopolistic foreign firms merely exploit new markets by capturing the "commanding heights" of local economies without diffusing the latest technology in poor countries. Therefore, arguments about technology transfer to local firms have been questioned. MNCs venture abroad to capture more and more market share for products that are becoming obsolescent in the more mature markets; therefore, valuable technology diffusion cannot be taken for granted.

Yet, again, others claim that the MNC will seek to expand abroad when the costs of "arms-length transactions" exceed direct investment (Caves, 1982). Thus, with lowered transportation costs and better means of communication, firms have an incentive to venture abroad because the costs of arms-length transactions exceed the cost of moving production close to the market. Caves also tried to explain MNCs, which are "horizontally integrated," with similar logic in terms of the need to minimize the transaction costs associated with correctly gauging the value of intangible assets, such as managerial talent and having to deal with new technologies that force adjustments of production to economies of scale.

Some of the explanations discussed above come together in the "eclectic paradigm," which has become a dominant way of thinking about the spread of FDI (Dunning, 2001). According to this view, companies have ownership-specific advantages they wish to exploit relative to their competitors. The more ownership advantages of firms cf from their competitors, the more they are likely to engage in foreign production given that they can exploit their ownership-specific advantages by expanding abroad. Thus, the spread of FDI can be predicted by knowing these advantages and what it is the individual firm is trying to capitalize on vis-à-vis the competition. In general, MNC activity can be characterized as market-seeking, or demand oriented FDI; resource-seeking, or FDI that goes after a resource, such as natural and human resources that are immobile; efficiency-seeking FDI, which tries to maximize an efficient division of labor by augmenting capabilities abroad; and strategic-asset-seeking FDI, which buys up assets that will complement its ownership-specific advantages and deny such assets to competitors. This paradigm allows broad application of theoretical propositions to questions such as what types of firms go abroad, from what types of economies, and where they locate.

The nature of FDI expansion is important for determining the bases of arguments about whether or not recipients of this form of capital are better off with or without it. The common thread that runs through all these explanations is the notion that MNCs seek to maximize profits and minimize costs, something normally expected from a rational economic agent. These explanations, however, are interpreted by the optimist and pessimist positions on the issue of foreign capital's effects on host nations in entirely different ways. For example, liberals see the profit motive as positive because increasing competition will lead to increased efficiency, something that will also transfer to other areas with the spread of MNC investments. The search for profits and competition will lead to constant reinvestment and continued growth, the benefits of which will diffuse to local firms and enhance their competitiveness beyond the local markets.

The pessimists, however, argue that real market competition is often subverted precisely because of the profit motive. Since the nature of the Western MNC is oligopolistic, no real good in terms of competitive practices or real market competition can be expected. MNCs use their economic power as leverage to monopolize markets, contravening the rules. Moreover, without the regulatory capacity within poor states MNCs promote collusive behavior and not competition. Oligopolization of markets does not lend itself to transferring technology nor diffusing progressive capitalist principles associated with profit-seeking investment. Therefore, there will be little transfer of technology from MNCs to local firms.

Liberals have generally blamed conditions within LDCs, particularly government policies, for failing to attract foreign investment (United Nations, 1991; Romer, 1993). Today, liberal economists and modernization theorists argue that undue restrictions and outright expropriation of foreign capital by many LDCs have hurt rather than helped. They point to the success of the Asian and Latin American NICs, suggesting that LDCs do have policy options that can mitigate what some suggest may be harmful externalities associated with MNC investments (Gereffi, 1985; Grieco, 1985; Moran, 1985). Indeed, as some argued, "Increasingly host governments will force the multinationals to serve their interests . . . From this perspective one can argue that with the relative decline of American power and influence, a larger and larger share of the benefits of foreign investment will flow to the host government" (Gilpin, 1976). Further, the competition to invest created by the proliferation of MNCs totaling roughly 63,000 parent firms and 821,818 foreign affiliates in the LDCs, the amount of leverage available to host governments for obtaining the most favorable terms, is possibly increasing (UNCTAD, 2001: 242).

Liberals blame the problems of development on the internal processes, political institutions, and cultural inhibitors that exist within the LDCs. There is depressed private investment within the LDCs because the social environment is not conducive to it. Taking their cue from the studies of Emile Durkheim and Max Weber, modernization theorists argue that internal processes within LDCs thwart the modernization process (McClelland, 1961; Huntington, 1968; Webster, 1995). Some blame was placed heavily on the cultural inhibitors, the mental models that are unfavorable to change, such as the lack of an "achievement motivation" and culturally determined attributes that get in the way of coping properly with modernity. Such arguments have also resurfaced in recent times—apparently "culture matters" (McClelland, 1961; Harrison, 1985; Harrison and Huntington, 2000). It is argued that large parts of the developing world lack what Max Weber identified as the "Protestant ethic" for explaining the European miracle, ironically using Confucianism as the contrast. Today, cultural arguments hail the communitarian values of Confucianism for being the backbone of East Asian success.

Economists, while increasingly taking softer factors, such as cultural styles seriously, blame instead human capital. The failure of many of the LDCs came to be blamed on their inability to harness technology properly and adapt to changing social, political, and economic situations (Abramovitz, 1986). Thus, theories of economic growth now view "human-capital" and other socio-environmental variables, such as fertility rates, schooling, and degree of social capital, which measure societal efficacy, as being vitally important besides the standard economic variables. Indeed, human capital determines investment endogenously. New growth theory (or endogenous growth theory) is regarded widely as an important corrective to neoclassical growth theory because the latter assumed technology to be exogenous. New growth theory accounts for why predictions of convergence were unrealistic. Since there are increasing returns to new ideas and technology, convergence is not automatic, unless of course one accounts for human capital (Romer, 1986; Lucas, 1988). Indeed, cross-national empirical work finds that poorer countries do in fact grow faster than richer countries, but only for a given level of human capital (Barro, 1991).[7]

If human capabilities are explanations for why LDCs had problems with adaptation, some suggest they are also the key reason why capital flows to poor states did not take place in the volumes that neoclassical models had predicted. According to Lucas (1988), political risk, the most often cited reason why many LDCs have not seen the expected infusions of capital, does not explain why capital movements were similarly sparse during the colonial era when political factors should have mattered less. Simply put, these arguments suggest that LDCs suffer from the lack of capital and technology because of endogenous reasons such as human capital and social capability in general, apart from the problems associated with poor policies.

The issue of capability, for neoliberals, is also intricately linked to the issue of politics within the LDCs. As Gunnar Myrdal (1971) argued, the success of the Western countries was predicated upon societal consensus about "modernization." Accordingly, nations were built alongside dynamic political institutions, and more importantly, nation-states had already formed as rather homogeneous entities. In other words, political instability because of societal discord was largely absent. This pattern, unfortunately, is not applicable to LDCs where nation-building, modernization, and adaptation to changed economic and political conditions are a conscious (or even a self-conscious) task. This task is seemingly insurmountable because political institutions, social and cultural fragmentation, and a general lack of consensus inhibited the flexibility and discipline required for modernization (Todaro, 1977; Waldner, 1999). In fact, for many, the political instability itself emanates from modernization pressures because the institutions within most poor developing countries are inadequate to handle the societal demands of modernization (Huntington, 1968). I treat this subject more extensively in the following chapters.

On the problems of modernization, liberals are somewhat split about the salience of democracy for enhancing the economic prospects of LDCs. For many, the earlier enthusiasm for the notion that "all good things" such as wealth and political freedom "go together" waned, and some began to argue a "cruel choice" between the creation of wealth and democratic governance (Bhagwati, 1966; Huntington and Nelson, 1976). Political and economic theorists who adhere to the liberal credo, however, do not generally share this view with equal intensity. Nevertheless, many liberals have been willing to blame internal political upheaval and instability for development problems and have emphasized sociopolitical stability for creating economic growth, even at the expense of democracy. Many take comfort in the notion that democracy comes in the wake of economic development; hence authoritarianism is perhaps a small, temporary price to pay for prosperity (Huntington, 1991). Today, however, democracy is viewed as intrinsically valuable and the issue of democracy and growth has gained added salience given that the recent democratic gains are highly dependent upon how democracy is able to deliver economic goods—consider the recent removals of democratically elected leaders from office in Pakistan and the Philippines because of widespread dissatisfaction with corruption and economic mismanagement. I examine the issue of democracy and development in greater detail in the following chapter, particularly focusing on the issue of qualitative aspects of democracy that are instrumentally and normatively valuable.

The neo-Marxist theories of underdevelopment

By the 1960s and 1970s, a critical social paradigm had emerged out of the neo-Marxist, or dependency, perspective, to challenge the rather deterministic views on development expounded by neoliberal, modernizationist perspectives. The neo-Marxist dependency theorists questioned the validity of the cultural theories of modernization that tried to explain development failure in the postwar era as being endogenously determined (Valenzuela and Valenzuela, 1978). These theorists, hailing largely from within the LDCs, questioned the Western bias and ethnocentrism of neoliberal theories on economic development, blaming instead the structure of the capitalist system itself for perpetuating underdevelopment. The problems for the LDCs were determined from outside. They argued that the trajectory of industrial and social development of the West cannot be superimposed on the South, as historical conditions are different for poor countries, given the West's structural dominance.

The early dependency theorists came primarily from the Latin American region, aiming their critiques at US "imperialism." There is clearly no one unified body of dependency theory, nor a clearly articulated position that is accepted by all, but André Gunder Frank, Samir Amin, and Immanuel Wallerstein are perhaps the most influential and theoretically most closely allied. Their views are clearly opposed to the modernization and Marxist (diffusionist) paradigms. They may loosely be termed "structuralists" because of the theory's emphasis on the capitalist world system's structural barriers against development in LDCs.[8]

Taking their cue from theories of imperialism, dependency theorists blamed instead the "unequal exchange" taking place between the North and South. According to this view, unequal exchange was predicated on the basis of the dominant position enjoyed by the advanced industrial countries and the resultant dependency of the poor countries on the rich. This perspective was so far reaching that by the mid-1970s it had galvanized the LDCs as a powerful bloc against global liberalism. Most poor countries seemed to be unified as a third-world bloc in such groups as the Nonaligned Movement and the Group of 77, which called for more economic autonomy and sovereignty for national development and initiated a call for a "New International Economic Order," which would make the world system less biased against poor countries (Krasner, 1985).

The core of dependency theory evolved around the structural analysis of the "world-system" perspective propounded by the sociologist Immanuel Wallerstein (1974), who suggested that a world capitalist system had emerged around the 15th century to structure the interactions among the members of the modern world system. Countries were not independent territorial and social units but were part of a single logic. The capitalist world system is marked by the formation of a distinct "core" group of states located in Western Europe and extended to North America and Australasia that enjoyed structural power vis-à-vis a weaker periphery. Thus, the structure of the capitalist world system apparently determined the position of peripheral status where the capitalist "core" was responsible largely for the continued peripheralization of noncore areas, perpetuating its own power and wealth. This peripheralization happened in various ways, but core capital came to be seen as instrumental in this process. Indeed, the capitalist "core" was directly responsible for the underdevelopment of the periphery because the system worked at the behest of core capitalism (Baran, 1962; Frank, 1969). Since MNCs were driven by the logic of "capturing" more and more market power, they were the girders on which the capitalist world system rested.

The process of underdevelopment of the periphery by the core was explained as one resulting from exploitation by the strong of the weak. Even though formal colonialism had ended, poor countries remained at the mercy of market forces determined by former colonial masters. In effect, colonialism was merely the formalization of this system of unequal exchange, which seemingly continued even after formal colonial control ended. For instance, because the structural power of the system was biased in favor of the core, advanced states acquired cheap raw materials from the poor nations and sold goods to the poor at value added prices. In fact, the Economic Commission for Latin America's (ECLA) widely published report on North–South trade under the leadership of Raúl Prebisch, which demonstrated steadily declining terms of trade for Southern primary commodities against Northern manufactures, gave dependency thinking a massive boost. Accordingly, the long-run terms of trade between North and South were supposed to benefit the North at increasing rates, reflecting the structural biases of the world capitalist system. In general, neo-Marxist theories rested on the foundations of Hobson's and Lenin's theories of monopoly capitalism and imperialism (Todaro, 1977; Menon and Oneal, 1986).

As noted already, neo-Marxists linked the issue of foreign capital investment within LDCs to the theory of unequal exchange by viewing foreign direct investment as an indirect and subtle form of the continuation of colonial exploitation. Ironically, however, classical Marxists had long recognized the progressive nature of international capital. Karl Marx was an early observer of the creative and progressive influences of foreign capital. Marx and Engels wrote, "The bourgeoisie, by the rapid improvement of all instruments of production, by the immensely facilitated means of communication, draws all, even the most barbarian nations into civilization . . . In one word, it creates a world after its own image" (1972: 339). Later Marxists, such as Lenin, Bukharin, and Luxemburg, however, argued that the export of capitalism would not necessarily develop the periphery smoothly. They argued that new contradictions leading to new tensions would arise between the ruling and working classes, especially as a result of the monopolization of capital within the industrialized countries. Even so, it was generally agreed that "the imperialist phase of capital accumulation . . . comprises the industrialization and capitalist emancipation of the hinterland" (Palma, 1995: 155).[9] It was also argued that peripheral societies could escape capitalist exploitation by getting rid of direct colonial control and its political structures. It was the vestiges of feudal, colonial political structures, not capitalism, that was to blame.

Noting the little progress that was actually achieved by the LDCs after decolonization, however, the neo-Marxist, dependency writers, diverging from pure Marxist arguments, began to argue that "modern imperialism" has evolved by way of a special historical process (Baran, 1962; Frank, 1969). In opposition to the early position that political emancipation would end colonial exploitation, they suggested that imperialist control continued indirectly through new, subtler, means. In other words, the old edifice of imperialism (the structure) continued to determine the fate of the LDCs, and dependency theorists contended this factor was what was the direct cause of the underdevelopment of poor countries (Baran, 1962; Emmanuel, 1969; Frank, 1969; Dos Santos, 1970). Unlike neoliberal modernizationists who looked within poor countries to find deficiencies, they argued that the blame lay outside.

For most dependency theorists, the form of postcolonial control and exploitation of the poor by the rich has direct and indirect effects, which underdevelop emerging societies in the periphery. First, there is direct exploitation because of a biased structure, through trade, aid, and direct investment. Second, the effects are indirect through the co-optation of segments of the society within poor states, those who are the elites that are part and parcel of the ancien régime and now working at the behest of colonial masters. The internal elite, who benefited from continuing ties with the metropole and of MNC capital, willingly participated in the exploitation of their own states. The MNCs exploited poor states by expropriating the surplus directly and with the collusion of the local elite. In this way, colonialism was perpetuated in new and more insidious ways. The national bourgeois could not independently develop as a bulwark against "imperial control" because they were co-opted into a system of exploitation that was aimed at their very own. The ruling classes within LDCs came to be seen not as a "dynamic" bourgeois moved to action by the competitive, progressive forces of capitalism that Marx had observed, but parasitic rentseekers, part and parcel of the oligarchic structures imposed from outside, structures preventing free and fair markets and impeding the development of a democratic path to industrialization (Frank, 1969). In this way, dependency theorists linked the global system of capitalism both to economic underdevelopment and to the democratic deficit; but the causal mechanism for both was international capital and structural bias on a global scale.

The structure of the MNC, wherein strategic decisions were made at the headquarters about issues of profitability, thwarted real partnership and determined investment decisions by local subsidiaries and affiliates, which only reflected the interests of the headquarter countries and not of the hosts. MNCs used their superior knowledge of business practices to avoid taxation and to expropriate excessive profits through devious methods, such as "transfer pricing" (Lall and Streeten, 1977; Gilpin, 1987). The "triple alliance" between the MNC, host government, and the local elite, whom Johann Galtung referred to as the "bridgeheads" of the capitalist system, acted to distort economic development to the detriment of the larger peripheral societies (Galtung, 1971; Evans, 1979). All of these harmful features about MNC activity in LDCs apparently diminish the levels of human welfare in the host economies.

Noting the considerable development that has been achieved by the newly industrialized countries in Latin American and Asia, many observers offered alternative explanations of classical dependency theories. These alternative dependency theorists came to be called "dependent-development" theorists or "unorthodox" dependency theorists (Cardoso and Faletto, 1979; Evans, 1979; Bornschier and Chase-Dunn, 1985; Bradshaw, 1988; Cardoso and Fishlow, 1992). While acknowledging that development with MNC penetration was possible, these observers argued that new forms of dependency had developed, highlighting especially the deleterious effects of the "triple alliance" on income inequality. Foreign investment was supposed to expand the manufacturing base of the economy, mitigating the harmful effects of dependence on primary commodity exports, but in the process, MNCs captured the "commanding heights" of the economy, distorting the development process so that it led to a process of "uneven development" (Krasner, 1985: 81–94). Foreign capital, according to some was creating a "new international division of labor" where wealth was being created unevenly within LDCs.

Investment by MNCs was, therefore, thought to cause "disarticulated" economies because their activities did not spread evenly within a given society, precluding the "linkages" that permit autonomous development and giving rise ultimately to a "stagnant" economy characterized by "dualism." Even some orthodox economists referred to "immiserizing" growth stemming from similar processes. The disarticulation of the economy was manifested in highly unequal sectoral inequalities, where only the elites who were connected to the world system benefited by the core–periphery interaction while some others actually were left worse off. The resultant inequality also brought with it other harmful manifestations such as class tensions, political violence, rebellion, and crime (Boswell and Dixon, 1990; Jenkins and Schock, 1992; Rothgeb, 1996). The issue of inequality in particular became highly salient to those interested in explaining the lack of democracy in the developing world, especially among those states which had reached levels of socioeconomic development that made them conducive to inaugurating and maintaining democracy (O'Donnell, 1973). Accordingly, dependent development did not bring with it conditions expected by modernization theorists, but it brought instead "bureaucratic authoritarianism." Thus, foreign direct investment, even when promoting such good things as growth and economic modernization, could not deliver the goods in terms of "real" development, a result of which was inevitable stagnation over time.

In terms of democratic governance, dependency theorists of varying positions would agree that the problem of development in LDCs was the lack of democracy (Cardoso and Faletto, 1979; Evans, 1979). Since the major source of misery in the developing world was determined by forces from outside, most dependency theorists were not inclined to blame internal processes, but rather the instruments of the international capitalist system—the capricious national bourgeois and MNC investments. These reactionary instruments of the world capitalist system colluded to thwart democracy and perpetuate their own narrow interests (Frank, 1969). The causal chain, moreover, was clearly specified in many cases: MNC investments → lowered economic performance/income inequality → authoritarianism → underdevelopment. Poor countries remained poor and undemocratic because this served the greed of international corporations and local elite.

Many dependency theorists, at various stages, offered a wide variety of explanations as to how MNC investment harmed LDCs. These ill effects or, in economic parlance, "negative externalities," harmed those states that overly relied on foreign capital for their development strategies. While much of the literature was polemical, caught up in the larger global discourse of superpower rivalry, many academic voices apparently identified systematic links that drove some of the theoretical discourse. Foreign capital apparently harmed LDCs through displacement of local investment capital; MNCs introduced unsuitable and obsolete technology that was inappropriate for labor-rich poor countries; they altered indigenous tastes and practices that had unintended social consequences leading to instability; and they created unemployment problems, rather than easing them. Most insidiously, MNCs were to blame for the rise of authoritarian governments because policies that allowed corporate tax evasion, held down wages, cracked down on civil society organizations, such as labor unions and pro-democracy movements, and cut back social spending and public investment were institutional necessities for the MNC.

The rapid decline of the level of formal democracy among the decolonized LDCs in the 1960s, US military intervention around the world (ostensibly in the guise of anti-communism), and overt involvement of foreign corporations in the overthrowing of democratically elected governments in places such as Iran, Guatemala, Chile, and other countries, lent great credence to these sophisticated theoretical arguments. These clear prescriptions of how FDI was associated with underdevelopment offered by dependency/world-systems theories led to the conclusion that LDCs must disassociate themselves from the global trade and investment system, or in the words of Samir Amin, "delink," from the global capitalist system in order to prevent themselves from becoming "maldeveloped."[10] By the 1970s, the MNCs came to be seen as the chief instrument of capitalist exploitation, the "hidden hand" of international capitalism. Much of the thinking about MNCs also coincided with a wave of expropriations of foreign corporations within much of the newly independent states of Asia, Africa, and Latin America.

The proposition that the dependence of LDCs on multinational capital stifles both economic development and democratization is a two-way link offered by dependency theory as to why poor countries stay poor while the rich get richer. These arguments are clearly echoed by pessimistic voices on globalization and go beyond the polemical discourse generated during the height of the Cold War. According to a recent study on the subject, "Since new forms of foreign capital inflows to developing countries often are associated with a larger program of market-oriented reforms, these problems of transitional incompatibility between political and economic reform can make democratization significantly more difficult" (Armijo, 1999b: 22). Further, the highly plausible theoretical links identified by dependency theories have clear implications for debates on regime types and economic growth because FDI conditions the regime type within which it operates. According to one recent study, "*Foreign business* enhances its direct influence in an emerging market only through foreign direct investment. Once installed within the country, MNCs become local political actors" (Armijo, 1999b: 31; emphasis original). Moreover, Armijo (1999b: 35) pointed out the ambiguities associated with what exactly one might expect from FDI for democratization and autocratization, since the intermediate variable is whether or not there was growth. The argument is that both forms of government will be legitimized given economic improvement (Przeworski and Limongi, 1997). The question then is, *ceteris paribus*, which interaction is bound to be most effective in terms of improved economic performance? If, for example, as in China and much of East and Southeast Asia, growth is being driven by large infusions of foreign capital, is it that economic growth models that incorporate regime type misidentify foreign capital's positive effect on growth as an authoritarian effect given that these models do not control for FDI and domestic investment separately—in other words, is authoritarian growth due to FDI and not with any inherent virtue connected to authoritarian governance, except that authoritarianism is conducive to "stability"? On the other hand, if FDI promotes authoritarianism and thereby prevents democratically determined economic growth, studies that try to gauge the impact of democracy on growth will not capture the so-called negative externalities that may be attributed to FDI, which mask democracy's true effects on growth. These questions are not merely "academic"; they are crucial for answering the critical issues raised in the debate on globalization.

The issue of democracy and FDI and growth depend much on whether or not FDI has an affinity for authoritarianism. In an age of near universal appeal for democracy (at least procedurally) and without the context of superpower rivalry and geopolitical struggle between blocs, perhaps FDI's relation to regime type needs reevaluation. During the Cold War, the US and other OECD countries offered credits to MNCs to invest in strategically important countries, which were in fact often authoritarian and sometimes unstable (Schneider and Frey, 1985; Oseghale, 1993). Others find that when including the OECD countries, MNCs are no more prone to invest in authoritarian regimes than within democracies (Oneal, 1994). The picture is certainly not clear.

Moreover, the empirical evidence on whether or not FDI "causes" authoritarianism has proved to be highly inconclusive (Bollen, 1983; Bollen, 1988; Gasiorowski, 1988). Others have argued that FDI sometimes serves to cause democratization through its effects on the development of a national bourgeois class that is independent of the local political state (Becker *et al.*, 1987), while dependency theorists have argued that the national bourgeois forms a "comprador" class that works to stifle democracy (Cardoso and Faletto, 1979) and causes "bureaucratic authoritarianism" (O'Donnell, 1973). On the other hand, some have made rational-choice type arguments to show how FDI acted to deter the Peruvian military from movements to reintroduce authoritarian measures in that country (Stepan, 1978).

Kenneth Bollen (1983: 478) concluded that the question of whether or not dependency retards democracy depends on whether or not it does so indirectly through its effects on economic development. I pursue this issue further. Since the theoretical links between authoritarianism and foreign capital are usually made through foreign capital's effects on economics, it is further reason to investigate foreign capital and democracy's effects on economic growth independently of each other and interactively.

Most studies on democracy and growth, particularly the influential studies of Robert Barro (1998) and Przeworski *et al.* (2000) in the fields of economics and political science have not incorporated concerns relating to the differential impact of FDI, which in turn shaped endogenous factors such as the quality of governance. The issue of democracy and growth, therefore, is intimately linked to how FDI and democracy relate to each other. This study incorporates FDI separately in its evaluation of democracy and growth and addresses questions relating to democratization in the presence of FDI. The larger problem I address is to empirically evaluate the extent of the contradiction that pessimists on globalization invoke between FDI and democracy.

Causality between FDI and democracy

Questions of whether or not globalization will promote or harm development, thus, are intricately linked with the question of whether or not democracy and the market (capitalism) are compatible. According to one scholar on the subject, "the extent to which globalization has hindered or assisted democratization is a major issue of the day" (Munck, 2002: 4). The optimists see limited government involvement in the economy as favorable for increasing prospects of democracy because it allows alternative nodes of power within society. Stronger protection of private property rights and the

development of private bases of taxation lead to calls for a greater representation and voice in policymaking (no taxation without representation).
Contrarily, heavy state involvement in the economy is seen as dangerous to
"freedom" as it concentrates power in the hands of vested interests and
destroys social pluralism (Weitzman, 1993). Economic competition goes
hand in hand with political competition, driving efficiency and enhancing
prospects for strengthening democratic political institutions (Baghwati,
1993; Berger, 1993).

On the other hand, some see market capitalism as providing inordinate
power to narrow interests that have an incentive to subvert democracy and
markets, destroying social equality, communitarian values and pluralism.
According to one of the foremost theorists on democracy, Robert Dahl,
capitalism and democracy exist in a kind of "antagonistic symbiosis"
(Dahl, 2000: 166). This statement conveys, on the one hand, the idea that
capitalism and democracy are symbiotic, but also antagonistic. The debate
on globalization is in essence about this symbiosis and antagonism. Dani
Rodrik, a highly respected, orthodox economist, offered one of the best-
recognized warnings on globalization, which essentially suggested that the
reliance on liberalization, particularly on free trade, would undermine the
capacities of states to cushion society from the vagaries of a global free
market, destroying the bases on which "social consensus" rests. In other
words, democracy itself will be threatened by the social frictions uneashed
by globalization, further undermining chances for development (Rodrik,
1997; Rodrik, 1998).[11]

Theories of democratization usually emphasize the notion of countervailing power as key. Such power raises the cost of monopoly of political power
(Dahl, 1971; North and Weingast, 1989; Przeworski, 1991; Vanhanen,
1997). As such, the issue of rising social pluralism, generally associated
with the development of the bourgeoisie as a result of industrialization, has
taken a prominent place. Such theorists as Karl Wittfogel, William Kornhauser, and Robert Dahl point out the importance of pluralistic society for
balancing out interests and avoiding hegemony as vital for the emergence
of democracy (Wittfogel, 1957; Kornhauser, 1959; Dahl, 2000). Wittfogel
argued that in hydraulic society, the source of despotism was the concentration of the means of production in the hands of a few, allowing total power,
whereas the emergence of a multicentered society based on a more complex
division of labor made democracy possible. Others relate the emergence of
democracy specifically to the market. As Göran Therborn has written,
"Freedom of trade and industry created a network of divisive competitive
relationships . . . The market replaced the hierarchical pyramid of medieval
and absolutist feudalism. And it was in this unity-division of the national
state and market that the process of democratization originated" (Therborn, 1977).

Scholars have offered numerous reasons as to why and exactly under
what conditions democracy has emerged in recent times, such as defeat in

war, economic hardship, and changing international conditions, but much empirical evidence supports the general proposition that social conditions foster pluralistic structures, where monopoly of power is limited; and where industrial development and economic prosperity exist, democracy exists (Huntington, 1991; Burkhart and Lewis-Beck, 1994; Vanhanen, 1997; Przeworski *et al.*, 2000).[12] However, if modernization theorists see FDI as contributing to increasing the market and competitive forces, dependency theorists view FDI as working differently in developing countries. They accuse FDI of constraining market competition by pursuing oligopolistic rents and monopoly profits. Moreover, FDI directly affects authoritarianism by supporting autocrats who would act on their behalf. Developing countries may experience different effects from market forces, since they experience "dependent capitalism" owing to the domination of their economies by powerful MNCs (O'Donnell, 1973; Therborn, 1977; Cardoso and Faletto, 1979; Evans, 1979).

Currently, the pessimists on globalization echo arguments implicit in these older arguments stemming from theories of (under)development. They suggest that the conditions being imposed on weaker states by those who control capital are exploitative. They argue that since the lines between what is domestic and what is international are becoming increasingly blurred, the poor will be left defenseless, individuals and groups not conforming to the logic of globalization will have no champions, and democracy itself will be stunted. In other words, while state and individual sovereignty decrease, it is argued that "global capital" will become master (Gill, 1995; Korten, 2001). Even the recent spread of democracy and the emphasis on the rule of law are seen to be processes by which the powerful countries and corporations "make the world safe" for private and transnational capital at the expense of the majority of poor (Willett, 2001). Contrarily, others suggest that multinational corporations, which are sensitive to consumer demands in rich countries, are likelier to respect "human rights" and support open political conditions out of self-interest. Some recent evidence suggests that FDI is negatively associated with human rights violations controlling for other important factors, yet the question of formal democracy remains open (Apodaca, 2001; Richards *et al.*, 2001).

What about trade? FDI and trade generally go together. This is particularly true for the 1980s and 1990s, when formerly closed economies opened up and were keen to attract FDI because of highly constrained opportunities for borrowing following the debt crisis. In fact, for the entire 1970–99 period, we obtain a correlation of r = 0.47 between the ratio of trade to GDP and the stock of FDI and GDP. Therefore, the arguments about FDI and democracy are as valid as they are for trade, particularly with regards to its effects on economic growth and industrialization. While there is much evidence today to suggest that freer trade does indeed create higher economic growth (Frankel and Romer, 1999; Srinivasan and Baghwati, 1999;

Dollar and Kraay, 2000), the exact links of the direction of causality from trade to democracy and vice versa are still quite ambiguous.

Many find the trade-to-GDP ratio to be correlated with lower corruption (Ades and Di Tella, 1999; Gatti, 1999; Wei, 2000), which is one indicator of institutional development, but corruption does not proxy well for democracy per se—consider the recent removal of elected leaders from office in the Philippines and Pakistan because of widespread corruption. Besides, the direction of causality may very well be reversed—less corruption causes increases in trade. In general, liberals expect free trade to promote competition and liberal norms that promote democracy. According to some (Sandoltz and Koetzle, 2000: 44, 46), free trade promotes democracy by "intensifying economic competition, reducing the opportunities for corruption . . . and socializing actors into the predominantly Western norms of the international economy."

While the liberal view on trade and democracy go together, others make explicit links from political freedom to higher trade liberalization. Verdier (1998) traces this line of reasoning "back to Kant, Bastiat, and the British radicals, who believed that republics . . . were more likely to engage in trade than absolute monarchies." Some explain the "rush to free trade" as resulting from the recent wave of democratization. Since free trade benefits larger segments of the population, democracy encourages free trade by constraining rent seeking, the monopoly profits of vested interests (Milner and Kubota, 2001). Recently, Mansfield, Milner, and Rosendorff (2001) provided a rational choice-based link to democracy's direct causal effect on free trade. They explained the choice to engage in free trade as a function of voter desire to have low-cost, high-quality goods that come with free trade, as opposed to powerful interest groups that resist increased competition by currying the favor of an autocrat. Democratic politicians must listen to voters in order to maximize their chances of reelection. The instauration of democracy increases the likelihood that free trade increases (see also Penubarti and Ward, 2000).

Yet, the case of causal direction is not clear-cut, since it is widely believed that adjustment to free market conditions requires authoritarian regimes for suppressing dissent, even if temporarily, since the losers have strong incentives to scuttle reform (Haggard and Kaufman, 1992). The fact that many democratic nations including the United States practice trade restrictions means that trade does not at all times and places enjoy clear "majority" support.[13] Consider the debate in the US over NAFTA and the constant haggling between the major trading partners of the world (Burtless *et al.*, 1998). Moreover, rich country publics seem to have an enormous appetite for agricultural subsidies, despite the fact that agriculture is a minute part of most industrial economies. In fact, political economy models show that voting and lobbying activities can result in protection as well as liberalization (Grossman and Helpman, 1992). Whether or not democracy is more receptive to trade may depend heavily on factor proportions, where poor democracies may be more receptive to trade because they are labor abundant (Tavares, 1998). Regarding trade and democracy, just as with FDI, the question of direction of causality is an empirical one. I think the evidence is important for instructing global policies regarding the proper sequence for achieving democracy and economic prosperity in an age of globalization, and I address the issue with the latest available data in Chapter 5. First, however, I tackle the empirical issues and controversies surrounding FDI and growth.

3 Globalization and growth empirics

Introduction

As much of the discussion in the previous chapter suggests, the debate on the effects of foreign capital investment within LDCs has progressed largely along polemical lines, caught up in the ideological battles of the Cold War. This is particularly true regarding the arguments on FDI and economic development where the gulf between economists and the other social sciences (political science and sociology in particular) was greatest, and was generally the case until the appearance of a large body of empirically oriented research within sociology and political science that ostensibly demonstrated negative effects of FDI on growth in econometric studies— hard data that supported dependency arguments (Bornschier, 1980; Bornschier and Chase-Dunn, 1985). These studies demonstrated what seemed to be conclusive evidence of many of the case-study-based arguments about dependency. Bornschier and Chase-Dunn's results seemed to have solved the puzzle of the incongruity between what economists thought of FDI and the contrary views of structural theories of exploitation.

According to Bornschier (1980) the problem lay in differentiating the effects of short-term flows of capital from their long-term (accumulated stock) effects, and the results depended on how measures of FDI were operationalized. Flows were just new infusions of capital that boosted growth momentarily, but the structural impact of flows were negligible compared with the long-term accumulated impact of stock. Long-term accumulated stock, however, was theoretically the better proxy of the degree to which an economy was "penetrated" by MNCs, thereby a better measure of the MNCs' structural power over the host economy and polity. The ratio of accumulated stocks, however, could be large relative to the size of most LDCs. Evidence quickly mounted over a decade of research, largely in sociology and political science, that used the measure of FDI penetration (PEN) to address issues from dependency and mortality, fertility rates, other indicators of human development, to civil conflict. PEN research, as this genre of research came to be called, purported to find many of the dependency effects highlighted in the literature. These studies concluded that, "While the more 'primitive' forms of exploitation such as capitalist slavery, capitalist serfdom, and formal colonialism have disappeared, they have been replaced by . . . the hierarchical organizational structures of the modern transnational corporation" (Bornschier and Chase-Dunn, 1985).

I now turn to the empirics of this genre of research, highlighting important criticisms. I address the shortcomings of this research, build on the latest evidence, and bring to bear the most recent data and a sounder operationalization covering a longer period of time than previously tested by similar studies. Addressing this issue with the latest available data is crucial given that much PEN research relied on FDI stock data collected over three decades ago.

Capital is not capital!

Before Bornschier (1980) and Bornschier and Chase-Dunn (1985), the empirical evidence on FDI and growth as theorized about in the sociological and political science literature was extremely mixed and inconclusive. Indeed, their studies came to be regarded as "prototypical" of dependency research, and it synthesized many of the disparate dependency arguments. Bornschier is credited with having initiated an entire research tradition that examined foreign capital penetration on growth and other measures of human welfare. This genre of research continues to give enormous credence to the pessimistic voices on development under conditions of neoliberal restructuring and spreading international capitalism.

Bornschier and Chase-Dunn (1985) contended that the inconclusive results of previous studies on foreign capital and economic growth were due mainly to the improper conceptualization of foreign capital investment relating to dependency. While the flow of foreign investment has positive effects on growth, the penetration of LDCs by MNC over time causes negative, long-term growth, since it takes time for the negative externalities of foreign capital dependency to manifest themselves. The long-term harmful effects of foreign capital "penetration" are expected to occur by way of the many exploitative MNC practices already observed by dependency researchers. They argued that one main avenue by which MNCs exploit LDCs is specifically through the mechanism of "decapitalization" of peripheral economies. Decapitalization takes place directly as a result of MNC repatriation of profit and indirectly as a result of the effects of disarticulated economies on income inequality and domestic savings. The problems were deemed to be so serious that these researchers advocated the establishment of an international organization to govern the activities of MNCs (Bornschier and Chase-Dunn, 1985: ch. 10).

The widespread acceptance of Bornschier and Chase-Dunn's findings was largely due to their operationalization of the differential effects of flows and stocks on growth. Penetration gauged the influence of foreign capital within an economy independently of the rate of investment of new capital. In other words, penetration was a measure of the structural hold of foreigners on the economy, measured as the ratio of FDI stock to GDP (the total size of the economy). Bornschier and Chase-Dunn contended that separating the two effects of foreign capital was the key to understanding their differential effects and the reason why previous attempts at testing this issue had proved to be inconclusive.

Bornschier and Chase-Dunn based their analyses on theories of the MNC, which characterized the MNC as an oligopolistic economic actor (Vernon, 1971; Hymer, 1972). These theories described the MNC as a "vertically integrated" firm governed by the dictates of the "product cycle" and driven to seek oligopolistic rents in new markets. As discussed above, these theories viewed the growth of FDI not as a function of the free market forces whereby capital relocates to areas of high rates of return in search of new profits. Instead, FDI is a means by which large, rigidly organized corporations "control" markets for their own monopolistic profits, the end result being that peoples in the headquarter countries benefit at the expense of the poorer host countries. The structural power of the MNC gives it power over host-country markets so that it captures the "commanding heights" of the domestic economy and prevents indigenous development. The desire to perpetuate monopolistic profits prevents reinvestment of earnings and the expansion of economic activities by MNCs, which results over time in unrealized markets within LDCs. Bornschier and Chase-Dunn argued that MNCs repatriate profits to take out more than they brought in without leaving a trace of their activities in poor economies—these are the mechanisms of underdevelopment.

Contrary to the orthodox economists' view that governments, not foreign companies, are to blame, Bornschier and Chase-Dunn argued that host governments are generally powerless to control MNCs. The MNCs, which are technologically and organizationally superior to the weak, often internally divided, LDCs, have distinct advantages in their dealings with their hosts. They can easily circumvent the weak regulatory laws in their path and are hard to monitor by state authorities. This organizational superiority allows them to use undesirable methods, such as transfer pricing, to evade the host government's taxes. The economic power of the corporation also allows it to win powerful political favors when dealing within institutionally weak LDCs, so that what little regulation is possible is also by and large avoided through bribery and corruption. Bornschier and Chase-Dunn suggested that all of these factors make it quite unreasonable to lay blame on internal political conditions, but that MNC practices ultimately work to the detriment of LDCs, which despite even well-meaning laws are unable to control the repatriation of capital in the long run, leading to decapitalization of the economy and lower economic growth.

The eventual repatriation of profits, goods, and services, the terms of which are set in the core-country headquarters, and the exploitation of increasingly cheaper labor in the South (the export of the proletariat), enhance the overall welfare of the home countries while creating inequality abroad. Accordingly, MNC penetration does not enhance the balance of payments prospects of the poor host governments. These factors and others are the processes by which core–periphery interaction serve to further the underdevelopment of the periphery (Bornschier and Chase-Dunn, 1985). In the long run, then, even though there may be short-term growth spurts as a result of the inflow of capital, the long-term effect is of depressed domestic savings, leading ultimately to lowered investment and growth—dependent development is transitory.

Bornschier and Chase-Dunn's thesis takes into account one other harmful way in which MNC penetration affects economic growth. According to them, while MNC penetration creates inequality between the rich and poor states, it is also to blame for the inequalities that exist within societies. Income inequality within the periphery is affected through the alliance between the host-country elite and the MNC. The MNC is assured of cheap labor by the governing elites who suppress labor movements and foster low-wage policies. According to Bornschier and Chase-Dunn, the privileged in the periphery are integrated into the world system in stark comparison with, and at the expense of, the marginalized majority. The periphery's upper classes consume luxury goods to keep up with the bourgeois lifestyles of the core, adding to the gradual impoverishment of the capital-poor host country (Bornschier and Chase-Dunn, 1985: 120). Thus, decapitalization, which has enormous implications for sustained economic growth, takes place overtly as well as covertly, and the culprit is the MNC. For these reasons, the effects of foreign capital on economic growth have to be gauged in terms of both new investment flows and accumulated stocks—it is MNC "penetration" of host economies that is bad for LDCs, even if short-term flows cause some "growth."

PEN empirics

Given subsequent criticisms of PEN research and problems associated with Bornschier and Chase-Dunn's seminal work, and given that I will be replicating previous work to make my results as comparable to the others as possible, it is vital to understand aspects about the models and data of previous work. As discussed earlier, the novelty of Bornschier and Chase-Dunn's study lay in the fact that they attempted to distinguish between the flow of foreign capital and accumulated stocks as they affect economic growth. They defined the crucial independent variable, MNC penetration, as the share of MNC capital in the total stock of available capital within a given economy weighted by population size. Their measure of foreign capital flow is the difference between the stock of foreign investment between 1973 and 1967, divided by total Gross Domestic Investment stock between the years 1965 and 1970. They controlled for the effects of gross domestic investment because of its influence on prior investment flows and on economic growth. Their dependent variable, growth, is the percentage increase of per capita GNP between 1967 and 1973.

Their economic growth model followed a simple neoclassical growth model in which they controlled for the effects of convergence as expected by neoclassical growth theory. Thus they included the logged level of initial income, adding a squared term to account for any nonlinear shape of the growth trajectories of nations in the presence of foreign capital. The initial level of development controlled for the "ceiling effects" present at higher levels of development that were expected to produce smaller percentage increases in growth. They also included the level of exports divided by GDP to control for the extent to which a nation is integrated into the world system, and a logged value of total GDP to measure the size of the domestic market, or domestic demand, which is thought to stimulate growth.[1] The size of the domestic market is an important control variable, since Bornschier and Chase-Dunn argued that part of the negative effects of decapitalization stems from a small market size in LDCs where domestic demand is constrained. Their results may be summarized as follows:

1   FDI flows have a beneficial impact on growth, a finding consistent with orthodox economic theory, but penetration (stock of foreign capital relative to domestic investment stock in 1965) shows a negative effect on a world sample (n = 103).

2   Foreign capital penetration of core countries (n = 15) shows a positive effect, supporting the capitalist world-system theory, which argues beneficial effects from core–core interaction, but flow is negative, albeit statistically not significant.

3   Foreign capital penetration of LDCs, excluding the core (n = 88) shows a statistically significant negative effect on growth, but it is positive and significant for flow as it was for the world sample.

4   The division of the LDCs according to region, size, and level of development shows a net positive effect of initial flows of FDI, but negative effects for penetration. The small negative effect of penetration on the smaller African countries is interpreted to support the position that the size of the market determines the extent of integration into the capitalist system. Thus, Africa is seen to have escaped really harmful effects because of the lack of foreign capital in Africa compared to other LDCs.

These findings taken together apparently confirm the propositions of dependency theorists, especially those of the "associated dependent-development" school that argued that development was possible with foreign alliances but would result in distortions of the economy with harmful manifestations in the longer term. The negative effect of foreign capital penetration in the long run, despite the positive effects of flow,

apparently proved the hypothesis that MNC penetration leads to decapitalization, creating balance of payments difficulties for the host country,
thwarting further investment, and thus perpetuating underdevelopment.
Bornschier and Chase-Dunn concluded that

> Following an initial growth spurt [FDI] will create an industrial struc-
> ture in which monopoly is predominant, labor is insufficiently
> absorbed, and there is underutilization of productive forces. The
> peripheral countries that adopt this path of uneven development based
> on income inequality and foreign capital imports will experience eco-
> nomic stagnation . . . relative to countries that are less penetrated by
> transnational corporations.
> (Bornschier and Chase-Dunn, 1985: 39–40)

As noted earlier, a host of similar studies, utilizing the data published by
Bornschier and Chase-Dunn, found that the penetration of foreign capital
was responsible for a number of maladies in developing countries. The
problems attributed to foreign capital penetration ranged from high mortality, high fertility rates, low food supply, rebellion, etc. (London, 1988;
London and Williams, 1988; Boswell and Dixon, 1990; Wimberley and
Belo, 1992). These studies importantly differentiated the so-called MNC
"penetration effects" from "flow effects," finding deleterious effects of
foreign capital penetration on various forms of socioeconomic and political variables. Invariably, this body of literature became sizeable enough to
dominate the discussions on the subject of development within sociology
and political science (Firebaugh, 1992; Seligson and Passé-Smith, 1998).

Controversy

There were several early critics of the Bornschier studies, which were
mainly focused on the specifications of their models. Erich Weede (1981)
and Weede and Tiefenbach (1981) challenged the dependency perspective
on MNC penetration and its effects on growth and income inequality in a
systematic way. According to Weede and Tiefenbach (1981) and Weede
(1986a), Bornschier (1980) failed to control properly for intervening variables on economic development when evaluating the effects of dependency
variables on inequality and growth. They added, for example, a military
participation ratio (MPR) as an intervening variable and found no support
for the dependency position on MNC penetration. There was some early
evidence challenging the robustness of the results on MNC penetration
and growth, but these studies were extremely sparse (Jackman, 1982). No
significant theoretical nor methodological progress was made by the early
critics.

   This was generally the case until Glenn Firebaugh's (1992) devastating
reanalysis of Bornschier and Chase-Dunn's study. He demonstrated serious

flaws in the operationalization and logical interpretation of their results. Firebaugh demonstrated that Bornschier and Chase-Dunn (1985) had mis-interpreted their findings because they had used both foreign flow and stock in the same regression equation. The problem lay in the way in which flow and stock were constructed and entered the regression equation. The flow of foreign investment was positively correlated with growth, as neo-classical theories predict; but stock, holding flow constant, seemed to have a negative influence. Firebaugh demonstrated that the so-called harmful effects on growth were merely denominator effects stemming from the way in which flows and stocks were calculated. Since the rates of increase in foreign investment (flow), by definition, equals flow over stock, the greater the initial level of stock, holding flow constant, the lower the growth rate. When Bornschier and Chase-Dunn report a positive effect on flow and a negative effect of stock, they are simply finding that slower increases in foreign capital are associated with lower growth, hardly a controversial finding. To demonstrate the problem, Firebaugh used the same data as PEN researchers to reestimate the relationship between foreign investment and growth, approaching the problem differently.

For comparability, Firebaugh's model closely resembled the PEN research models on growth. His reanalyses yielded results that showed that both foreign and domestic investment rates are positively associated with growth, but domestic investment rate is more strongly associated with growth.

As Table 3.1 demonstrates (column 2 eq. 2) an annual investment rate of 1 percent of foreign capital would lead to an increase in growth by 0.076, while the same percentage increase of domestic capital would boost growth by 0.233 percent. Firebaugh concluded that there was no evidence of a harmful effect of foreign investment, but he noted the "differential productivity" of the two forms of capital. His results indicate that domes-tic capital is approximately three times as productive as foreign capital. While not harmful, the lower productivity of foreign investment hardly made it seem an important engine of growth. Firebaugh (1992: 122) con-cluded, however, that there is "no evidence in the PEN data of a general tendency for foreign investment to retard growth."

Firebaugh's analyses showed logically how PEN research and, more specifically, Bornschier and Chase-Dunn's pioneering study on the effects of MNC penetration on growth, are based on misinterpreted results. His tests of whether or not foreign investment decapitalizes or augments domestic investment found no evidence of "decapitalization" upon which depen-dency arguments hinged. Several studies were quick to challenge Firebaugh's conclusions (Dixon and Boswell, 1996a; Dixon and Boswell, 1996b; Kentor, 1998). Dixon and Boswell (1996a) posed the most cogent counter-arguments, questioning Firebaugh's operationalization. Arguing that what has gone "unnoticed" beneath Firebaugh's critical remarks of capital dependency research is the serious issue of the differential effects of foreign and domestic investment. They claimed that this differential effect is sup-

Table 3.1 Firebaugh's results for foreign and domestic investment rates on economic growth, 1967–73

	(1)	*(2)*
Foreign investment rate:		
Coeff.	0.077†	0.076†
t-value	3.6	3.6
St. *b*	0.33	0.33
Domestic investment rate:		
Coeff.	0.233†	0.233†
t-value	3.8	3.9
St. *b*	0.36	0.36
PEN controls:		
Size:		
Coeff.	0.56*	0.56*
t-value	2.2	2.2
St. *b*	0.25	0.25
Exports:		
Coeff.	0.004	0.004
t-value	0.30	0.30
St. *b*	0.03	0.03
1965 GNP/c (log):		
Coeff.	0.87	0.63
t-value	0.20	1.1
St. *b*	0.17	0.12
[Log (1965 GNP/c)]²		
Coeff.	−0.05	
t-value	−0.04	
St. *b*	−0.05	
Adjusted R²	0.51	0.52

Sources: Adapted from Firebaugh (1992: 112–13)

Notes
Adjusted R^2 w/o control variables = 0.42, n = 76 LDCs
* denotes $p < 0.05$ (two-tailed)
† denotes $p < 0.01$ (two-tailed)

portive of the dependency position first highlighted by the pioneers of PEN research, which was the different impact of flows and stocks and the accumulation of long-run differential effects.

They claimed that the large differential effects of the productivity of domestic and foreign investment (favoring domestic by approximately a three-to-one margin as reported by Firebaugh) support the dependency claims that there are long-run adverse effects through all the "negative externalities" associated with greater investment from foreign sources over domestic counterparts. Dixon and Boswell interpreted the differential productivity of the two forms of capital as the process of "disarticulation" in action (Dixon and Boswell, 1996a: 545). In other words, they investigated the possibility that, when foreign capital increasingly penetrates the economies of developing countries, it carries with it "negative externalities" that are harmful in the long run. They reiterated some of these externalities, such as overurbanization, tax avoidance by MNCs, rising income inequality, the weakness of linkages, and, most importantly, the crowding out of domestic capital, all of which have been identified by dependency scholars in the past as being deleterious for LDCs.

As these new studies pointed out, the large differential effect between foreign and domestic investment reported by Firebaugh suggests that foreign capital is clearly inferior. Moreover, they faulted Firebaugh for not explicitly considering the issue of foreign capital "penetration," since Firebaugh used only rates of investment (flow) in his studies and did not crucially test the effects of accumulated influence of FDI on an economy (stock), such as that which Bornschier and Chase-Dunn had tried to do in their studies. They take issue with Firebaugh for not addressing properly the question of "penetration" of foreign capital, which is after all the crucial dependency variable. According to Dixon and Boswell, penetration, as the definition of the term is commonly applied, is a gauge of the stock of foreign capital relative to the stock of domestic capital, or, in general, a measure of the influence of foreign capital within an economy (Bornschier and Chase-Dunn, 1985: 60–2). Penetration, therefore, must be defined by a measure that captures the influence of foreign stock in relation to the size of the economy or as a ratio of domestic capital. Firebaugh's tests of the investment rate, therefore, say very little about the relative influence of foreign capital within an economy as understood in dependency terms or world-system theories. For Dixon and Boswell, it is the "drag effect" of foreign penetration that is crucial and not just the rate of increase of foreign capital. Thus, Firebaugh's model was merely a flow model.

Dixon and Boswell expanded on Firebaugh's study by considering both "differential productivity" and "penetration" effects of foreign and domestic capital on economic growth, while accounting for the shortcomings of earlier studies as noted by Firebaugh. They retained the investment rates measures and the model tested by Firebaugh, but now included the critical measures of MNC penetration defined as the ratio of FDI stock to GDP and FDI stock to domestic capital stock. They proposed to gauge the effects of foreign and domestic investment rates on economic growth while holding foreign capital stock (penetration) constant. In other words, they tested the effects of the relative size of each sector's (foreign and domestic) capital mix while accounting for the differential productivity of the two forms of capital.

Their results are presented in Table 3.2. As seen there, adding the measures of foreign capital penetration to Firebaugh's model consistently yields a negative coefficient for foreign capital penetration. They also included a

Table 3.2 Dixon and Boswell's results of capital penetration's effects on economic growth, 1967–73

Foreign penetration For. K 1967 / Total K 1967	−0.07* (−2.6)			
Foreign penetration For. K 1967 / GDP 1967		−0.02* (−2.4)	−0.03* (−2.3)	
Foreign investment rate 1967–73	0.07† (3.4)	0.07† (3.6)	0.08† (3.6)	0.07† (3.6)
Domestic investment rate 1967–73	0.26† (4.4)	0.23† (4.0)	0.22† (3.5)	0.23† (3.8)
Log (size)	0.37 (1.5)	0.46 (1.9)	0.58* (2.3)	0.45 (1.8)
Log (GDP/pc 1965)	0.02 (1.5)	0.02 (1.5)	0.01 (0.50)	0.02 (1.5)
Exports (Exp./GDP 1965–73)	0.94 (1.7)	0.94 (1.7)	0.75 (1.2)	0.90 (1.5)
Domestic capital penetration (1967 K/ GDP 1967)			−0.003 −(0.6)	0.001 (0.2)
Constant	−3.36† (−3.1)	−3.72† (−3.3)	−3.16† (−2.7)	−3.78† (3.3)
Adjusted R²	0.55	0.55	0.51	0.54

Source: Adapted from Dixon and Boswell (1996a: 552).

Notes
Entries are unstandardized OLS estimates with t-ratios in parentheses; n = 76 LDCs
* denotes $p \leq 0.05$ (two-tailed)
† denotes $p \leq 0.01$ (two-tailed)

model with domestic capital penetration together with the foreign capital penetration measure and found that only foreign PEN is negative and statistically significant. Their conclusion based on these results is that "while holding investment rates constant, as foreign capital increasingly penetrates Third World economies, the countries in our sample experience slower rates of economic growth" (Dixon and Boswell, 1996a: 553). Based on these results, Dixon and Boswell theorized that LDC economies with larger shares of foreign capital suffer from "negative externalities" that impede economic growth. In the subsequent debate between Firebaugh (1996) and Dixon and Boswell (1996b), neither side yielded any ground. According to Dixon and Boswell (1996b: 561) "more recent cross-national data on investment rates and penetration must be gathered to test the theory under current global economic conditions and to undertake more stringent analyses." In order to address this complex question, it is necessary first to examine some of the shortcomings of the controversial research just discussed.

Firebaugh and Dixon and Boswell have considerably advanced our understanding of the effects of foreign capital on economic growth. However, all these studies suffer serious shortcomings. First, all of them use foreign investment stock estimates collected more than three decades ago by Ballmer-Cao and Scheidegger (1979), who warned that their investment stock values are "only estimates and must be used with caution." Questions about the data extend beyond mere impressions, because Dixon and Boswell's results for domestic capital penetration (Table 3.2) are not significantly associated with growth. This result is hard to swallow given the strong evidence suggesting that, of all the variables thought to influence growth, it is investment that is most robustly correlated with economic growth (Levine and Renelt, 1992). Can it be that domestic investment stock, which is by far the largest portion of investment in most countries, has no effect on growth? These facts warrant closer examination of the issue with more recent data.

The most important criticism of the previous studies, however, is that they have exclusively used simple neoclassical models of economic growth, which are inadequate. The model used by Bornschier and Chase-Dunn, Firebaugh, and Dixon and Boswell merely controls for the standard PEN variables, which approximate a simple neoclassical growth model, without controlling for human capital. In the simple neoclassical model first constructed by Robert Solow (1956), an economy producing a single output exhibits constant returns-to-scale in production and diminishing marginal productivity of both labor and capital. The model, thus, predicted that convergence between rich and poor would occur given decreasing returns to capital and the deepening of capital within LDCs. The deepening of capital is simply that increases in the capital-to-labor ratio above the population growth rate would increase productivity and wages. Given factor mobility, or the movement of capital and labor to areas of highest returns, the capital-to-labor ratios and factor prices will move toward equality.

In Solow's model, however, technology is treated exogenously, and the model assumes perfect market competition. Since labor mobility is restricted in the real world, mobile capital and technology were expected largely to do the equalizing. This was the process of convergence that was now formalized mathematically. Yet, empirical analyses of the convergence effect predicted by Solow actually showed that the opposite was happening—no convergence, but divergence in income per capita (DeLong, 1988; Pritchett, 1997).

The failure to find evidence for convergence drove new growth theorists, or endogenous growth theorists, to argue that capital deepening was not the whole story of economic growth. Since models accounting for investment in physical capital explained only a small portion of the variance in growth rates, it was plausible that the growth of population would decrease the capital-to-labor ratios, hence of per capita growth and the rate of convergence. Further, since there was evidence to suggest that growth decreased fertility and that increased fertility dampened investment, there were positive feedback effects of low population growth on the growth of per capita income (Becker and Barro, 1988). In other words, countries' per capita income did not grow, because the gains in capital-per-worker were shared among more workers, and the more children per household the lower the investment rate because of the rise in consumption. Thus poorer countries did not converge because their real incomes did not keep pace with population growth.

Moreover, endogenous growth theorists also argue that viewing technological change as purely exogenously determined is unsatisfactory. These theorists, following Paul Romer's (1986) seminal article, base their arguments on increasing returns-to-scale as a factor of the existing level of human capital. Accordingly, technological change did not occur purely as a function of the amount of capital invested but was also influentially determined by the level of available human capital. As Romer (1993) conceptualized it, some countries suffer from both "object gaps" and "idea gaps," which taken together explain the wide variations in growth performance. In other words, investment in physical capital with low levels of learning is analogous to buying computers without knowing how to use them. To stretch the analogy further, the productivity gains from computers come only with the human capability that is able to run them and depend on the quality of the ideas that are applied to computing power.

Empirical analyses of the determinants of economic growth that took into account endogenous factors found that augmenting the simple neoclassical growth model with human capital variables, such as education and health, predicts growth and convergence strongly (Barro, 1991; Blomström *et al.*, 1992; Levine and Renelt, 1992; Mankiw *et al.*, 1992; Grossman and Helpman, 1994; Barro, 1996; Temple, 1999). More recent empirical and theoretical work by economists on the issue of foreign capital and growth also seem to suggest that foreign capital's interaction with favorable socioenvironmental conditions, especially education, does matter to a far greater degree than capital's effects alone (Lucas, 1990). To use Romer's (1993) analogy again, "objects" and "ideas" must interact for maximum productivity. A recent empirical analysis of 69 LDCs for the 1970–89 period found that the flow of FDI is not significantly correlated with economic growth, controlling for the initial level of development, human capital in the form of educational attainment, government consumption, and a proxy for market distortion, but the interactive term of FDI and human capital is significantly positively associated with growth, supporting the notion that foreign capital's benefits are maximized in its interaction with the "absorptive capability" of technology that foreign investment brings (Borenzstein *et al.*, 1998).

Likewise, others report a synergistic relationship between FDI and human capital. Blomström *et al.* (1992) found foreign capital's direct effect on growth to be almost twice as strong when testing just the higher-income developing countries as opposed to the entire sample, suggesting that foreign capital works better among the more "advanced" countries. These findings also point to the fact that foreign capital works best where there is a high degree of human capital. The conclusions of Blomström *et al.* are that "a certain threshold level of development is needed if the host countries are to absorb new technology from investment by foreign firms" (1992: 23). Although both studies mentioned above supply important clues as to how foreign capital benefits LDCs, it is not directly comparable to the empirical analyses conducted in the PEN research tradition and the recent critiques of it because of the crucial differences associated with the flow of investment and the stock of accumulated capital. This is generally true of analyses among economists, who focus on new investment, and other social sciences, such as sociology and political science, which pay attention to the influence of stock, given the theoretical import of dependency or world-systems theories that dominate development studies.

Adjudication: new data and models

All of the studies discussed above as PEN research have generally tested a short period of time covering the six years from 1967 to 1973, a time frame determined by the availability of the older data. This study builds on de Soysa and Oneal (1999), who used newer FDI stock estimates and tested the 1980–90 decade. In short, they found no effects of MNC penetration on growth covering this new period. They reported results on the rate of investment, which are almost identical to the others, but they pointed out a serious misinterpretation about the differential effects of foreign and domestic capital. They demonstrated that the size of the coefficients is determined by the ratio of foreign to domestic investment stock, which favors domestic by 13 to 1. Their reanalyses showed that the right comparison of FDI and domestic investment—the dollar for dollar comparison—favored FDI by roughly five times. When others claimed FDI to be less good, therefore, they were really saying that $13 of investment was better than $1. They also showed that FDI and domestic investment were conditioned by the availability of human capital.

The present study extends earlier analyses to cover the entire three decades from 1970 to 1999, using the latest, updated FDI stock and flow data reported by UNCTAD (2001) and World Bank (2001). It accounts for new growth theory more stringently than the previous studies, measuring the extent to which FDI is influential at three points in time, 1970, 1980, and 1990, on the growth rates of FDI over the 1970–80, 1980–90, and 1990–8 periods, following as closely as possible the previous tests of this issue. Essentially, I extend de Soysa and Oneal (1999), keeping as closely as possible to the controversial studies discussed above, to make my results comparable with others.

In our recent efforts to update data and collect time-series data for the present study, several problematic areas in the UNCTAD data were discovered, which warrant reanalysis of all previous studies, including our own (de Soysa and Oneal, 1999). First, UNCTAD data are constantly updated. More importantly, however, UNCTAD has revised much of their earlier estimates of stock, particularly for many African countries because of new procedures in collecting and verification of accuracy. As the notes to the data indicate, the FDI stocks have been verified for accuracy with national sources and official websites for almost all countries for the first time since UNCTAD began collecting these data, resulting in some substantial revisions presented in the latest version (UNCTAD, 2000). Further, I discovered that for a host of economies for which stock was estimated by summing flows, the FDI flows reported in current dollars summed to the value reported for stock, an unlikely coincidence. It seems that UNCTAD unfortunately reported stock figures that were constructed with flows in current dollars, without conversion to constant dollars.

This study reanalyzes earlier studies correcting as far as possible for these shortcomings in the data in the following ways. It uses the UNCTAD (2000) estimates of stock for 1980, which are now updated and presumably the most carefully screened estimates presented by UNCTAD. In order to get beyond possible problems in the way that UNCTAD may have accumulated stock, I convert the flows to constant dollars for all countries and create stock 1990 by accumulating flows reported by the World Bank (World Bank, 2001). Like the UN the World Bank also uses the IMF's balance of payment statistics for their flow data.[2] The changes in stock estimates are reflected in the correlations as the new foreign penetration score and the old reflect some difference ($r = 0.40$). The old foreign capital penetration scores are reported in de Soysa and Oneal (1999). However, the reestimated stock adding flows match those of the UN for the years 1990 and 1999 almost identically ($r = 0.98$). The stock estimates for 1980 accumulating flows from 1970 are correlated with the UN estimates of stock for 1980 at $r = 0.96$, which suggests that our data are almost identical to the UN estimates. We set all negative values of stock to zero, since by definition there cannot be negative MNC activity. Using these reestimated stock figures, this study reanalyzes the effects of FDI on growth following earlier studies. Besides the updated data, the current study analyzes panel data covering roughly three 10-year periods between 1970 and 1999. The control variables, which are similar to the PEN studies and controversial empirics reported in Firebaugh (1992, 1996) and Dixon and Boswell (1996a), are reported below.

In order to adjudicate the controversial studies by Firebaugh (1996) and Dixon and Boswell (1996a, 1996b), I first reanalyze these studies with the newer data covering the period 1970–99. To isolate the effects of the new data, I retest Firebaugh's investment rates model. Following others, I calculate change in foreign and domestic stock in the decades from 1970 to 1999 as the annual rate of change. This is the variable that Dixon and Boswell reported as well. The annual percentage change of foreign capital stock from 1970 to 1980 is derived as: $[(^{10}\sqrt{(\text{Foreign } K_{1980}/\text{Foreign } K_{1970})}) - 1] \times 100$. The formula is repeated for the two other decades in the same way. The annual domestic investment rates are also calculated the same way. Domestic stock is estimated by adding flows using the same depreciation method as that used for FDI stock, adding flows since 1960 to estimate stock 1970 and then adding flows to stock estimate at 1970 to construct stock 1980, 1990, and 1999. The domestic investment flows are estimated by transforming yearly total investment flow data reported in the GDN data and subtracting FDI flows.

Another slight difference between this study's variables and the older studies is that I use total trade to GDP to proxy for world market integration rather than exports alone as others have done (Bornschier and Chase-Dunn, 1985: 92). While the correlation between exports and total trade are quite high, it has also been noted that there is little difference in the effects of both measures on economic growth (Levine and Renelt, 1992). In any case, total trade captures aspects of economic dependence and integration to a greater degree than exports or imports alone (see also Gasiorowski and Power, 1998). Moreover, several studies have found that total trade has positive effects on growth that are more significant than exports or imports alone (Dollar and Kraay, 2000). Total trade to GDP is measured as the yearly average between the three periods and is obtained from the Global Development Network's Economic Growth Data Base (Easterly and Sewadeh, 2001). The other control variables are the same as the PEN research variables introduced first by Bornschier and Chase-Dunn. The variables and data are discussed in detail below.

These tests are followed by a replication of the Dixon and Boswell modification of Firebaugh's study. The measures of foreign and domestic capital penetration are added to the basic investment rates model to test the crucial effects of foreign and domestic stock (penetration) on economic growth. In other words, these tests gauge the effects of MNC penetration in the initial year of the testing period. Following Dixon and Boswell, I define penetration as both foreign and domestic capital stock over GDP measured at 1970, 1980, and 1990, the initial years of the three decade panels. The replications of the Firebaugh and Dixon and Boswell studies are followed by specifications adjusted to capture human capital. The rationale is that the productivity of capital may be affected by the environments within which it locates and also because locational decisions of MNCs are affected by the socioenvironments within countries.

Most growth studies use secondary school enrolment, or years of schooling, as measures of human capital. Others have argued that human capital should be treated as more complex than simply education alone, but that health and the condition of women should be seriously considered. Fertility and mortality rates, for example, capture social conditions that affect growth independently of education, which improves the specification of growth models (Barro, 1998; Temple, 1999; McDonald and Roberts, 2002). Instead of adding proxies for education, mortality, and fertility separately because they are all highly correlated, a common factor using principal component factor analysis on school enrolment, fertility, and under-five mortality rates, is constructed. The three measures are clear proxies for the social environment and capture different aspects of human capital. They are also widely available (UNICEF, 2000; World Bank, 2001). The first component accounts for 88 percent of the variance in the three measures and the Eigen values confirm its validity. This component, which I call "human capital" is measured at the beginning of each growth period (1970, 1980, and 1990) and is made up of equal values of each of the principal measures. I transformed the values so that increasing human capital means increasing education and decreasing fertility and under-five mortality; its mean equals 0 by construction.

Most of the previous studies, following Bornschier and Chase-Dunn (1985), used a standard neoclassical growth model, which accounts for the investment rates, trade, the size of the domestic market proxied by total GDP to capture domestic demand, and the initial level of income to capture the theoretical expectations of convergence (poor countries grow faster than richer countries because of higher absorptive capability of capital, and richer countries slow down because of ceiling effects). Total GDP (market prices) and income per capita (PPP) at the initial dates of the three growth periods are obtained from the GDN data. I construct average annual growth rates by using per capita income reported in the GDN data and linearly fitting each year's values, following the World Bank's methods so as to minimize the effects of extreme points (World Bank, 2002b). I test the following equations:

$$\text{growth}_{it} = \beta_0 + \beta_1(\text{FIR}_{it}) + \beta_2(\text{DIR}_{it}) + \beta_3(\text{Trade}_{it}) + \beta_4(\text{Size}_{it}) + \beta_5(\text{Income}_{it}) + e$$

$$\text{growth}_{it} = \beta_0 + \beta_1(\text{FIR}_{it}) + \beta_2(\text{DIR}_{it}) + \beta_3(\text{Trade}_{it}) + \beta_4(\text{Size}_{it}) + \beta_5(\text{Income}_{it}) + \beta_6(\text{fpen}_{it}) + \beta_7(\text{dpen}_{it}) + e$$

$$\text{growth}_{it} = \beta_0 + \beta_1(\text{FIR}_{it}) + \beta_2(\text{DIR}_{it}) + \beta_3(\text{Trade}_{it}) + \beta_4(\text{Size}_{it}) + \beta_5(\text{Income}_{it}) + \beta_6(\text{fpen}_{it}) + \beta_7(\text{dpen}_{it}) + \beta_8(\text{humancap}_{it}) + e$$

Where FIR = foreign investment rate, DIR = domestic investment rate, Trade = trade-to-GDP ratio, Size = total GDP (logged), Income = initial income per capita (logged), and humancap = human capital

I use ordinary least-squares (OLS) estimation with Huber White corrected robust standard errors (Stata, 1999).

All previous studies, particularly the relevant studies discussed above used the cross-national method with one panel covering roughly a decade. This study looks at three 10-year panels in a cross-national design covering the period 1970–99. The total number of data points is roughly 247, with coverage of roughly 98 countries for which complete data are available on all of the variables measured at three points in time. Since the design of the data yields three points in time, serial correlation is presumably not a large problem. The most efficient and consistent estimates for this type of data setup (N-observations per panel is much greater than the number of panels), however, are the OLS linearization/Huber/White/sandwich estimates of variance. These variance estimates provide correct coverage rates to panel-level heteroscedasticity and are robust to any type of correlation within the observations of each panel (Stata, 1999).

Results of new analyses

Table 3.3 reports results of the basic investment rates models analyzed by Firebaugh (1992). The results with FDI stock estimates derived from my two methods of estimating stock and the UN's own estimates, are reported. The models with the UN data are only available from 1980 onwards, thus yielding only two panels. Column 1 reports results for stock estimated wholly by accumulating and subtracting flow data. As seen there, the results are consistent with previous analyses, whereby FDI investment rates and domestic investment rates are positively associated with growth and statistically significant—a percentage increase in FDI increases growth by 0.03 percent, whereas a percentage increase in domestic investment increases growth by 0.44 percent. The size of the market (proxied by total GDP) and trade-to-GDP ratio are positively associated with growth and statistically significant, and there is no discernible convergence of income between rich and poor countries—initial income is positive and statistically not different from zero.

As de Soysa and Oneal (1999) suggested, however, the smaller effect of FDI on growth must be compared with domestic investment on a "dollar for dollar" basis because 1 percent increase in FDI is not the same value as a similar increase in domestic investment. In fact, the median value of domestic investment stock is 39.6 times greater than the median value of the stock of FDI (see summary statistics in the Data appendix). The "dollar for dollar" comparison between the two coefficients is the ratio between the coefficient for domestic investment rate (0.44) and the product of the coefficient for the foreign investment rate and the relative size of the two forms of stock (0.028×39.6), which suggests that a dollar of foreign investment boosts growth 2.5 times more than a similar amount from domestic sources, a result similar to that reported by de Soysa and

Table 3.3 Reanalysis of foreign and domestic investment rates on economic growth, 1970–99

Variables	(1)	(2)	(3)	(4)	(5)	(6)
FDI investment	0.028$	0.040†	0.086$	0.032$	0.042$	0.070$
rate (FIR)	(2.9)	(2.0)	(5.0)	(2.9)	(2.7)	(4.6)
Domestic	0.44$	0.39$	0.53$	0.41$	0.37$	0.48$
investment rate	(9.5)	(7.4)	(8.9)	(9.5)	(8.1)	(9.6)
Ln size (GDP)	0.38$	0.42$	0.32$	0.26$	0.30$	0.24$
	(3.3)	(3.6)	(2.5)	(3.5)	(4.1)	(2.8)
Trade/GDP	0.008$	0.010$	0.005	0.006$	0.007$	0.004
	(3.7)	(2.7)	(1.5)	(3.7)	(3.1)	(1.6)
Ln initial	0.15	0.11	0.26	–1.6$	–1.6$	–1.4$
income/pc	(0.72)	(0.53)	(1.3)	(–5.0)	(–5.6)	(–4.7)
Dummy	–0.61*	–0.57*		0.38	0.44	
1970–80	(–1.8)	(–1.9)		(1.2)	(1.6)	
Dummy	–1.3$	–1.2$	–1.3$	–0.70$	–0.58†	–7.5$
1980–90	(–5.3)	(–4.8)	(–4.7)	(–3.4)	(2.6)	(–3.2)
Human capital				1.4$	1.4$	1.3$
				(6.7)	(7.6)	(7.6)
Constant	–7.0$	–7.1$	–8.1$	7.8$	7.5$	5.4†
	(–6.1)	(–6.1)	(–7.8)	(3.1)	(3.1)	(2.6)
F	37.7	26.7	32.1	51.9	42.9	45.9
p-value	0.0000	0.0000	0.0000	0.0000	0.0000	0.0000
R²	0.52	0.50	0.58	0.64	0.63	0.68
N	248	247	181	248	247	181
Countries	96	98	96	96	98	96

Source: Firebaugh (1992: 112)

Notes
Huber-White robust standard errors computed in all tests.
* denotes $p < 0.10$
† denotes $p < 0.05$
$ $p < 0.01$ (two-tailed)

(1) and (4) FDI stock 1980 obtained by accumulating flows since 1970 and subtracting flows to construct 1970 stock. Stock 1990 and 1999 obtained by adding flows to estimated stock in 1980 (depreciation considered)
(2) and (5) utilize FDI stock 1980 from UNCTAD (2001) used as benchmark from which FDI stock 1970 was constructed by subtracting flows and FDI stock 1990 and 1999 by adding flows (depreciation considered)
(3) and (6) utilizes FDI stock estimates reported by UNCTAD (2001) for 1980, 1990, and 1999 (only available for two panels as 1970 stock is unavailable).

Oneal (1999) in their cross-national test using a single panel covering the 1980s.

Column 2 shows results estimated with investment values derived using the UN's estimate of stock for 1980 and other stock values estimated by subtracting and adding flows. The results on all variables are little changed. The dollar for dollar comparison yields a 3.2 times advantage to FDI over domestic investment. In column 3, the coefficients of the variables of interest using the UN's estimates for stock (all points in time) are larger for FDI and the difference may be attributed to the smaller number of data points (only two panels, N = 181). The dollar for dollar comparison with the UN's stock estimates yields almost a five-to-one advantage for FDI. The results taken together show consistently that foreign investment rate is positive and significant for growth, and that, compared dollar for dollar, its effect on growth is substantially larger than investment from domestic sources.

The reported results demonstrate that the effect of FDI on growth does not seem to be driven by a particular way in which FDI stock has been estimated in previous studies. Interestingly, the results are extremely close to those reported by different studies over the decades using very different data and methods covering differing time periods. Moving along in Table 3.3 across columns 4, 5, and 6, results for equations including the human capital variable show that social conditions in terms of higher education, lower fertility, and lower under-five mortality predict growth significantly. Notice also very strong support for the convergence effect as predicted by new growth theory, where initial income is now negative and statistically significant—countries that were initially richer grew 1.6 percent lower on average over the three decades than poorer countries, but only for a given level of human capital as measured by our health and education proxies. The increased R^2 indicates better fit than the baseline model, and the models with human capital capture over 60 percent of the variance explaining economic growth. Given the similarity of results using differently estimated stock, I go on with only my preferred method, which is estimations using the UN's estimate of stock for 1980 as a benchmark. The results with these estimates are the closest to those reported by de Soysa and Oneal (1999) for the 1980s with a cross-section of 114 countries.

Table 3.4 reports results with the crucial measure of FDI penetration (FDI stock-to-GDP ratio) in the basic investment rates model, addressing specifically the debate between dependency studies and their critics as discussed above.

Looking across columns 1, 2, and 3, foreign capital penetration has no statistically significant effect on growth, contrary to the results reported by Dixon and Boswell (1996a) in their study using older data for the 1967–73 period. While FDI penetration is not significant, the accumulation of domestic stock relative to GDP predicted growth positively, a statistically significant result. These results too are highly supportive of de Soysa and Oneal's (1999) conclusions contradicting the pessimistic views of dependency theorists regarding foreign capital's role in economic growth.

Moreover, columns 4, 5, and 6 show that the interaction between FDI and human capital is positive and significant on growth, while the interaction between domestic investment and human capital is not significantly

Table 3.4 Reanalysis of foreign and domestic investment penetration on economic growth, 1970–99

Variables	(1)	(2)	(3)	(4)	(5)	(6)
FDI investment	0.041†	0.036§	0.034†	0.064§	0.036†	0.063§
rate (FIR)	(2.5)	(2.6)	(2.4)	(4.8)	(2.4)	(4.8)
Domestic	0.37§	0.41§	0.42§	0.43§	0.42§	0.43§
investment rate	(8.1)	(9.1)	(8.9)	(9.0)	(9.7)	(9.9)
(DIR)						
Ln size (GDP)	0.30§	0.28§	0.28§	0.27§	0.27§	0.27§
	(3.0)	(3.7)	(3.7)	(3.7)	(3.7)	(3.8)
Trade/GDP	0.008†	0.006§	0.007†	0.004	0.006†	0.004*
	(2.4)	(2.8)	(2.3)	(1.6)	(2.2)	(1.7)
Ln initial	−1.6§	−1.4§	−1.4§	−1.3§	−1.4§	−1.3§
income/pc	(−5.6)	(−5.7)	(−5.7)	(−5.8)	(−5.4)	(−5.9)
Dummy	0.43	0.92§	0.90§	0.89§	0.88§	0.89§
1970–80	(1.5)	(2.8)	(2.7)	(2.8)	(2.7)	(2.9)
Dummy	−0.59†	−0.089	−0.12	−0.17	−0.13	−0.17
1980–90	(−2.5)	(−0.33)	(−0.44)	(−0.70)	(−0.47)	(−0.68)
Human capital	1.4§	1.2§	1.2§	0.91§	1.2§	0.93§
	(7.7)	(8.0)	(8.1)	(5.5)	(4.5)	(3.7)
FDI stock/GDP	−0.0017		−0.0042	0.0049	−0.0040	0.0048
(PEN)	(−0.19)		(−0.47)	(0.61)	(−0.45)	(0.61)
Domestic		0.0043§	0.0044§	0.0034§	0.0044§	0.0034§
stock/GDP		(3.1)	(3.1)	(3.0)	(3.0)	(3.0)
(PEN)						
Human cap. ×				0.024§		0.024§
FIR				(3.5)		(3.5)
Human cap. ×					0.0087	−0.0017
DIR					(0.36)	(−0.07)
Constant	7.5§	4.9†	4.8†	4.0†	4.6†	4.0†
	(3.4)	(2.5)	(2.5)	(2.2)	(2.4)	(2.3)
F	38.1	40.9	38.0	38.6	36.8	38.4
p-value	0.0000	0.0000	0.0000	0.0000	0.0000	0.0000
R²	0.63	0.65	0.65	0.67	0.65	0.67
N	247	247	247	247	247	247
Countries	98	98	98	98	98	98

Notes
Huber-White robust standard errors computed in all tests.
* denotes $p < 0.10$
† denotes $p < 0.05$
§ denotes $p < 0.01$ (two-tailed)

The investment measures are derived by using FDI stock 1980 from UNCTAD (2001) as a benchmark from which FDI stock 1970 was constructed by subtracting flows, and FDI stock 1990 and 1999 by adding flows (depreciation considered).

different from zero. These results support the empirical work of others who show foreign capital to be conditioned by human capital (Borenzstein *et al.*, 1998). These results are somewhat different to de Soysa and Oneal (1999) who report both interactions as significant in the 1980–90 period. Perhaps the longer period of time covered by these data account for the insignificant effect of the interaction between domestic capital and human capital in the 1980s. In general, however, all results support previous studies that challenge dependency views on the effects of FDI on growth. Despite the use of three times as many data points in these analyses than those used previously in similar studies, the results are highly similar to de Soysa and Oneal's (1999) critique of PEN research and Firebaugh's (1992, 1996) conclusions about FDI and growth. FDI benefits LDCs!

4 Democracy and growth

Theory old and new

Introduction

Nobel laureate Mancur Olson (1993: 575) noted that "the moral appeal of democracy is now almost universally appreciated, but its economic advantages are scarcely understood." Przeworski and Limongi (1993: 51, 66) reviewed the literature extensively and concluded that this is a subject about which "social scientists know surprisingly little." They added that the topic is "wide open for reflection and research." As some point out, "how to govern for prosperity is likely to be the most important policy puzzle of the twenty-first century" (Bueno de Mesquita and Root, 2000). While theory and empirical evidence support the link between higher levels of income and democracy (Burkhart and Lewis-Beck, 1994; Diamond *et al.*, 1995; Brunetti, 1997; Przeworski *et al.*, 2000), the issue of whether or not democracy will allow increases in wealth is highly disputed, and empirical evidence inconclusive (Sirowy and Inkeles, 1991; Przeworski *et al.*, 2000).[1] There is apparently consensus that democracy does not promote economic growth, even if it does no harm.[2]

In the worst instance, Barro's (1996, 1998) influential empirical studies reported a curvilinear relationship between democracy and growth. He found that while a moderate increase in democracy may spur growth, further increases stifle it. Apparently, this supports the view that high levels of democracy lead to demands for redistributive policies that hamper the steady creation of wealth. According to Barro (1996), those who find positive direct effects of democracy on growth do so only because such studies fail to control properly for social factors intimately associated with democracy, such as schooling and health. Apparently, there is nothing about regime type that helps us predict growth net of the effects of the socio-environment associated with democracy, such as high human capital. Since human capital is theoretically linked to economic growth in new growth theories, or endogenous growth theories, positive effects of democracy on growth vanish when human capital is accounted for. Barro's (1998) analyses confirm the empirical validity of this assertion.

The question of democracy and growth is not simply "academic" but holds grave implications given that promise of economic prosperity provided much of the impetus for the "Third Wave" of democracy, and any "backwash" is surely contingent on the realization of this promise. The current scholarly consensus on democracy and economic performance offers little hope for optimism. This chapter demonstrates that the empirical findings of the cross-national literature upon which the current consensus rests do not distinguish between qualitative aspects of democracy that are theoretically relevant for economic growth and normatively valuable for the way in which we think about democracy. While previous measures used capture several important dimensions upon which our idea of democracy rests, these subjectively derived measures conflate several aspects of democracy that may cloud the important aspects that are theoretically relevant for why democracy should promote, or hurt, economic growth.

Identifying such aspects is not purely academic but also helps the clarification of how democracy should be conceptualized operationally. Given that institutional design may make democracy produce normatively differing qualitative outcomes, knowing the concomitants of these differing qualitative aspects of democracy can help policy that seeks to promote institutional design for making democracy work for its own sustenance. As many suggest, not all democracy is the same (Przeworski, Stokes, and Manin, 1999). Scholars in comparative politics identify two democratic qualities, or, in the words of some, two visions of democracy—one that clearly reflects majoritarian tendencies where power of governance is concentrated, and another that reflects proportional tendencies that increase the size of the governing coalition and diffuse power (Lijphart, 1999; Powell, 2000). Majoritarian democracy tends to concentrate power, while proportionality diffuses it, an issue that relates to representativeness, access to policymaking, and accountability, which are in turn related to theoretical questions on regime type and economic growth and normative debates about what exactly is democracy (Lijphart, 1999). As many argue, what might be crucial may not be regime type so much as it is the quality of "governance." Questions of the quality of governance are mirrored also in the larger theoretical discussions about the nature of democracy in normative terms, where a clear distinction is made between democracy in the "liberal" mold as opposed to "illiberal" democratic values that concentrate power, even if in the "people" (Holmes, 1995).

This study highlights why it is necessary to critically examine what goes into values of democracy that we use in models of economic growth. I argue that the issue of democracy's effects on growth is best examined by distinguishing "good" democracies from the "bad," at least in terms of economic growth. There is much subjectivity that goes into categorization depending on the tastes of each observer, but at least good and bad in relation to economic growth allow us some criteria by which to make objective judgments about desirable aspects of "democracy." In other words, I want to distinguish qualitative aspects of democratic structure, keeping with those who espouse the importance of institutional variation for the effective functioning of democracy, which in turn affects the quality of output (Huntington, 1968; Lijphart, 1993; Putnam, 1993). In other words, the institutional structures within which democratic politics take place affect processes that bear on policy and other outputs (Bueno de Mesquita and Root, 2000). As Alesina and Perotti (1994: 351) suggested, "economic policy is the result of political struggle within an institutional structure. The empirically oriented researcher and the policy adviser have to be well aware of how politics influences policymaking." As Elster *et al.* (1998: 97) remind us, "democracy allows different forms of democratic government."

In what follows, I examine the very heart of democratic theory to tease out what is "good" and "bad" democracy and how in fact institutional variation within democracy may influence economic policymaking in a growth-promoting direction. Moreover, I will argue also why such a vision of democracy in terms of the qualitative aspects associated with it is normatively better, since what it really means to live in a democracy is really about being able to participate meaningfully in the political life of a community, to have one's interests reflected in policy, and objections heard.

This study examines the question of regime type and growth by considering three main general links between political factors and economic performance. The first is represented by the problem of regime type and rent seeking.[3] The second comes from arguments about the quality of institutions and questions of property rights, and the third perspective is based on the nature of regimes and the coherence and quality of policymaking, particularly as it affects developing societies with less experience of its practice. While all three of these general perspectives are interrelated, they are analytically useful only if treated as being distinct. For example, if growth is only about property rights' protection, then economic freedom alone should determine economic growth, a testable proposition. From such a perspective, politics is largely missing, an omission that most neo-classical economists applaud.

On the other hand, economic freedom and the degree of rent seeking are interconnected. Coherence and quality of policy also relate to rent seeking and the issue of property rights, but they encompass more than just economic freedom: they include the way in which democratic politics in particular are structured, capturing the degree to which government is more or less representative, accessible, transparent, and encompassing. For example, how much "insulation" a government may have in terms of carrying out growth promoting policies depends on the consensual nature of the policy arena and on whose interests are truly represented and who is left out (Haggard, 1997). Such arguments are especially salient to the developing world where policy instability and the inability to adjust to better policy paths are a major factor determining performance. Recently, there has been much emphasis on institutions as the answer to the puzzle of regime types and growth, but institutions are not well connected in theory to the political nature of economic policymaking.

Mancur Olson (1982, 1993) has suggested influentially that economic growth (particularly among democracies) is influenced by social rigidities that come about because powerful groups are better organized to overcome collective action problems that allow them to engage in rent seeking, which results in constrained markets and lowered growth. He has suggested more recently, however, that the extent of this behaviour may depend on the quality of institutions. He writes, "the intricate social cooperation that emerges when there is a sophisticated array of markets requires far better institutions . . . than most countries have" (Olson, 1996: 22). Another Nobel laureate highlights the importance of institutions in a somewhat different light. According to Douglas North (1989), one of the foremost theorists on institutions and economic change, the neoclassical theory of economic growth is deficient because it does not take "transaction costs" into account. Neoclassical theory simply posits that growth is a function of available land, labor, and capital, or as being determined merely by population and savings, but assuming a "frictionless" world.

North (1989: 1319) suggests that "the costs of transacting are the key to the performance of economies" and a crucial omission in the neoclassical literature. According to this view, in simple societies individuals are faced with few transaction costs because societal norms of behavior and personalized networks of association afford the guarantees that are necessary for simple forms of economic exchange. In these settings, specialization and markets are limited and no written guarantees (such as contracts and constitutions) are necessary. In a more complex world, however, economic exchange extends far beyond the personal world of a tribe or clan, where production is based on specialization. Such a setting is characterized by specialized interdependence, where well-being is dependent on a complex system of exchange, but not necessarily involving repeated dealings that occur in close-knit societies. Under such conditions, according to North (1989: 1320), "costs of transacting can be high, because there are problems both in measuring the attributes of what is being exchanged and problems of enforcing the terms of exchange; in consequence there are gains to be realized in cheating, shirking, opportunism."

To minimize the ill effects of the costs of transaction, elaborate institutional structures have to be devised to constrain individuals from acting in socially harmful ways. For these reasons, effective markets require such devices as contracts, bonding of participants, brand names, copyrights, monitoring systems, and effective enforcement mechanisms. These are staple features within most developed societies, which are deemed therefore to have well-specified and well-enforced property rights.

With respect to property rights, the continuously democratic states of

Western Europe, America, and Oceania, especially the UK, the US, Canada, the Scandinavian states, and Australia and New Zealand testify to the success of economic development under continuously "democratic" conditions. Examining the prerequisite conditions for the industrial rise of England, North and Weingast (1989: 803) argued that it was the extension of strong property rights as a result of weakening sovereign authority that set the stage. They write, "the more likely it is that the sovereign will alter property rights for his or her own benefit, the lower the expected returns from investment and the lower in turn the incentive to invest." What is not clear from the proponents of the "democracies protect property rights" argument, however, is what institutions and processes in democratic societies achieve this end (Przeworski and Limongi, 1993). It seems that the answer from the above arguments is that constitutional government, which simply restrains power, is enough.

Such answers raise questions about whether or not democracy is necessary for protecting property. There is no clear explanation as to how democracy (excepting the procedural feature of elections) inherently safeguards property rights better than a dictator. Such a concern is even more problematic when thinking about developing countries, which by and large do not carry the same historical baggage as the industrialized countries, where democracy emerged as a result of a rising bourgeoisie due to early industrialization. In fact, some suggest that the crises of democracy among developing states after decolonization are attributable largely to the sequence of democratization. Mass participation occurred simultaneously with state building, leading to institutional incapacity (Eckstein, 1996; Huntington, 1968). The incorporation of mass society in the political life of nations led to various forms of state–society, elite–mass coalitional arrangements and bargains that led to growth retarding policies (Waldner, 1999). In other words, even democracy came to be abandoned because constitutions alone did nothing to constrain power and protect property, for example.

This third perspective is largely grounded in political science theories, development studies, and political economy of policy reform. This perspective is based on the notion that what matters for public-policy outcomes is not whether a regime is democratic or not, based on political leaders being elected to office, but rather how "democracy" works in practice in much of the developing world. Contrary to the naïve early expectation stemming from modernization theory that "all good things" follow each other to the point where social expectations are satisfied if people are allowed to express them, this perspective sees the problem for postcolonial societies as being unique as a result of low institutionalization of political life (perhaps as a result of the short experience of working with democratic rule). If institutions are crucial for social and economic stability as many believe they are, then what about democratic institutions makes them more efficient and what makes them less so? This question can be answered only by connecting democratic theory to normative aspects of democracy reflected in aspects that we value, such as the degree to which democracy allows choice in policy, access to its formulation and implementation, and the consensual and deliberative nature of the process. These theories have much to say about normative content regarding democracy in practice, shaped by its qualitative aspects. I examine these perspectives in greater detail below.

Despite the explosion of empirical analyses of regime type and economic growth, there has been surprisingly little discussion of the nature of the crucial independent variable—democracy.[4] Most empirically oriented, hard-data analyses uncritically use one or other standard measures of democracy, most of which are indices based on aggregated values of features of politics related to an idealized form of democracy, such as the degree to which executive power is constrained. This criticism is particularly true of the economics literature on growth. The most widely used measures happen also to be subjectively derived by way of expert coding, perhaps introducing large biases as to which aspects of democracy are given weight over which.[5] More importantly, however, aggregated measures, even if we disregard subjective biases, could obfuscate real effects of some essential features of democracy that normatively speaking should be emphasized over others, which may or may not be related to economic growth. Finally, a big criticism of some of the subjective measures is that poor economic growth itself may weigh in heavily in subjective coding, so that levels of democracy may in fact acquire values that are lower than warranted, based on performance.

This study uses objectively derived data that measures the degree to which democracy reflects "polyarchy." According to Robert Dahl (1971), one of the most cited theorists on democracy, polyarchy can be achieved along the two axes of the degree of contestation and inclusiveness (the degree of participation). This is explicitly a "governance" model of democracy, which is minimalist, but avoids all kinds of baggage which may come along with democracy that becomes overemphasized.[6] I will demonstrate that the qualitative features of democracy that may be measured along these two dimensions are of value in answering the question of regime type and economic growth, and that the inconclusive results of previous studies may in fact be driven by the measures of democracy most commonly used in similar studies. Democracy conceptualized along a dimension of polyarchy allows us to identify two distinct qualitative visions of democracy—the majoritarian vision, which concentrates power within government, and the proportional vision, which tends to diffuse power.

Arend Lijphart (1984, 1999) demonstrated forcefully that there are two distinct patterns of democracy—consensual and majoritarian—which differ qualitatively and yield different political, social, and economic outcomes (see also Powell, 2000). While he focuses mainly on the developed democracies, I feel the issues he addresses in this regard are especially salient for developing countries, particularly because the gap between rich and poor democracies on the two dimensions of polyarchy, inclusiveness and competitiveness, is much greater than the average gap between rich and poor gauged by other criteria defining democracy (I compare the hard data on this issue below).

I address the empirical analyses in at least three important ways compared with all previous studies. First, I formulate hypotheses based on theoretical literature on the nature of democracy and what aspects of it should have a positive impact on growth and which features impact growth negatively, using an objectively derived measure of democracy that captures these dimensions. Second, I account for human and physical capital more stringently than most analyses that find positive effects of democracy on growth, exploring further the nature of the curvilinear relationship between democracy and growth reported by influential empirical analyses within economics (Barro, 1998). Third, I account for physical capital investment more stringently that others, looking at rates and levels of both foreign and domestic investment. Given the higher growth impact of a dollar of foreign investment compared with a dollar of domestic investment (see previous chapter), it may matter that foreign and domestic investment rates be controlled independently when assessing the effects of regime type on growth. Since some argue that FDI prefers authoritarian regimes among the poor countries, I want to separate out the effects of regimes from that of outside influence more strictly. For example, was growth within the largely authoritarian regimes driven by higher levels of FDI there? It is crucial, therefore, to separate the effects of physical capital investment, because regime type may affect both endogenously and exogenously determined investment.

Regime type and economic growth

Sirowy and Inkeles (1991) distinguished three main perspectives on democracy and growth. The first, the "conflict" approach, finds democracy and development to be incompatible.[7] Development apparently requires authoritarian regimes, free of the burden of electoral demands and pressures to make the hard choices necessary for economic growth. This position is articulated most clearly in the work by Samuel Huntington and colleagues who criticized the early modernization literature for being too naïve about "all good things" going together. They argued that, as modernization progressed, the institutional capacity of developing nations was often overwhelmed by political demands and pressures from mass mobilization (Huntington, 1968; Huntington and Dominguez, 1975; Huntington and Nelson, 1976).

According to this view, democratic politics create enormous pressures for redistribution of wealth and for consumption rather than investment, a policy path inimical to long-term growth. The median voter, whose income is lower than the average income, will naturally vote to redistribute income.[8]

Moreover, democracies that end up in such bad political equilibriums are unable to effect necessary change. The transparency inherent in democratic politics does not provide progressive state agents sufficient insularity and cushioning from electoral pressures and demands, deterring successive governments from initiating "unpopular," but necessary, economic reforms and adjustments. Haggard (1990: 160) put it bluntly when he suggested, "in general, greater politicization will reduce the coherence of policy and the speed with which adjustment can be undertaken." As (Barro, 1996: 1) reminded us also, dictators rarely engage in central planning to satisfy demands for consumption at the expense of private investment. East and Southeast Asia's growth success, therefore, is attributed to the fact that the state was able to carry out its development goals without the pressure of mass participation.

Second, the "compatibility" perspective finds that democratically elected governments are likelier to be better governors. Since democracy promotes citizen involvement in politics, democracy should be associated with greater accountability and citizen control, where policy determining the extent of winners and losers in economic life is consensually arrived at (Rodrik, 1999). Because of their greater legitimacy and regularized system of succession, democracies promote economic growth by promoting greater investment, expansion of economic participation, and the protection of property rights. The protection of property is taken for granted because democratic polities ostensibly cleave to the rule of law. Party competition for securing the offices of government, moreover, serves to hinder monopolistic control of the economy by coteries of a powerful few (crony capitalism), insures proper provision of public goods, promotes broad market liberalization, equity, and insures broad-based economic participation. Such assumptions are inherent in new rational choice frameworks for explaining the "rush to free trade" in recent years, for example. Democratic publics will vote for parties who are pro free trade because publics want low inflation and access to cheaper goods and services (Mansfield *et al.*, 2001; Milner and Kubota, 2001). In other words, free peoples will transact freely, broadening and deepening markets. Moreover, the threat of punishment of political leadership will deter bad policy and the use of public office for private gain (Bueno de Mesquita *et al.*, 2000).

Third, the "skeptics" see no discernible connection between democracy and economic development—that is, economic growth may be independent of regime type, and differing forms of regimes may hinder or promote growth and development. Since many LDCs have achieved varying degrees of economic success under authoritarian, semidemocratic, and democratic conditions, some expound models of "developmental states" that share some common features that cut across regime types. Leftwich (1995: 435) proposed the following as distinguishable political characteristics of the typical developmental state:

1   it contains a determined developmental elite
2   it has relative autonomy
3   it contains a powerful, competent, and insulated bureaucracy
4   it contains a weak, subordinated civil society
5   it displays a propensity for repression

Notice that all the points noted above suggest that the developmental state facilitates elitist politics, contains an autonomous state in the hands of a "cushioned" bureaucracy, discourages an active civil society, and even allows repression. By definition, therefore, developmental states are certainly not the liberal democratic states in the standard conception of freely transacting individuals making the market that favors economic development. They contain instead a mixture of democratic and authoritarian features. Leftwich's criteria are illuminating in that they suggest that developmentalism is somehow harmed by the popular "politics" inherent in a politicized and mobilized public. The questions I address are as follows: Are all democracies so hampered? What indeed about popular politics is threatening? Are there forms of democracy that can mitigate the harm of populist mobilization, which of course does not happen in every democracy? Are there other features of democracy that diffuse power, force consensus, and represent the populace's wishes in the policy process without disregarding minority opinion?

The inconsistency of the findings of empirical studies linking regime type to economic efficiency has led many to argue that the key to this "empirical puzzle" is unlikely to be discovered by pursuing the subject as a question of regime type. Features of developmentalism may in fact be conflated with authoritarian features and certain harmful aspects of extreme forms of populism may be mistaken for being "democratic," at least in terms of the subjective evaluations of measures of democracy. Instead of viewing two types of regimes as containing opposite features to each other, some argue that differing institutional arrangements have differing effects on transaction costs and property rights, which in turn have a bearing on economic development (North, 1989). Indeed, Przeworski and Limongi (1993: 51) wrote, "political institutions do matter for growth, but thinking in terms of regimes does not seem to capture the relative differences." Many have begun to argue the importance of institutional strength within regimes with regard to their impact on property rights, the crucial link between differing regimes and economic performance (North, 1989; Olson, 1996).

Leblang's (1996: 3) study, admittedly the "first approximation" of the relationship between democracy, property rights, and economic growth, found that democracy and property rights form to provide complementary effects on economic growth, albeit not very strongly. He concluded in support of Joan Nelson's statement, "[a] good deal of attention has focused on regime type, but the contrasts between democratic and authoritarian regimes may be less important than some more precisely specified institutional variables that cut across types of regimes" (Leblang, 1996: 18). According to Haggard (1990: 4), "institutional variation is critical for understanding why some states are capable of pursuing the policies they do." This point suggests that it is not merely regime "type" that matters for growth, but certain features within regimes that facilitate adaptability to favorable conditions and provide the incentives and disincentives for favorable economic policymaking. As Haggard noted, "even if there were evidence that democracies outperformed autocracies, we would still be interested in explaining the wide variation among them" (Haggard, 1997: 121).

Given the arguments that institutions and property rights do matter, the issue of the quality of democracy becomes especially salient when assessing the relative advantages of democracies and autocracies. Lumping together all democracies as one type of regime in empirical analyses, therefore, is bound to yield misleading, or at best null, results.

Much recent literature finds that institutional variation among regimes is key to understanding the issue of whether or not regime type matters for growth (North and Weingast, 1989; Alesina and Perotti, 1994; Keech, 1995; Olson, 1996b; Weede, 1996; Leblang, 1997). Institutional quality is especially salient to the issue of predictability of policymaking, not in the sense of stability where bad policies are hard to change, but stability as in an absence of arbitrariness in the policymaking arena. Moreover, a neglected side of democracy and growth is the question of what facilitates flexible, consensual responses to rapidly changing economic situations and the qualitative aspects of responses by governments to the day-to-day policy matters demanded by a democratic polity.

More often than not, institutions are viewed as static and inanimate, devoid of political content. The standard views are that institutions provide security from intrusive government and insure the effective functioning of markets. Property rights are secure where institutions prevent arbitrary acts by government, providing a system of checks and balances, or a system of multiple veto points so that political power remains checked. Efficiency is a question of how well institutions perform and the extent to which rent seeking is prevented. Much of the discussion around differing forms of democracy has centered around presidentialism versus parliamentarism, focusing heavily on the developed countries. As some find, there is little heterogeneity among the richer countries where the presidential and parliamentary forms share many features in common and where outcomes may in fact be similar despite different organizational form (Moe and Caldwell, 1994; Tsebelis, 1995).[9]

Moreover, others have suggested that institutional effectiveness is mediated in part by cultural settings within which institutions function, a question that increases the complexity for addressing questions about regime type and growth. In other words, social norms, such as civic virtue and norms of reciprocity, and trust are also thought to be crucial (Granato *et al.*, 1996; Knack and Keefer, 1997b). My position, therefore, is to view qualitative aspects of structural variation in a more aggregated sense, where I distinguish between the two types of democracy broadly as being consensual and oppositional. I measure variations among democracies that may have differing impact on the many aspects of the good things mentioned above, such as countervailing power, veto points, flexibility of policy response, and, above all, social consensus, all of which influence growth. For example, how is growth affected if power of government is concentrated, as in the majoritarian systems? Are proportional systems where policy is more consensually arrived at better for growth? As the following discussion suggests, properly identifying how differing types of democracy should matter in efficient and stable policymaking with regard to growth should be clearly specified. If some dictatorships can promote production over predation better than others, why should this not be true between types of democracy also?[10]

The notion that regime type may not matter as much as structural variation within democracy is also suggested on the basis of the Weberian problem of "form" and "content" (Gourevitch, 1993). After all, the classical Greek philosophers such as Aristotle recognized that while dictators could work for the common good, democracies could very well work against it in the form of "mob rule." It is not clear as to how and why democracies, by mere virtue of containing institutional and substantive aspects of democratic governance, influence economics, or even good government. More contemporary analysts have also challenged the modernizationist notions that deterministically expected democracy to be compatible with other "good things" such as economic growth and development (Bienen, 1970; Weiner and Huntington, 1987).

"Elite" and "mass" systems are both likely to display features of democratic competition and autocratic repression, a highly salient point especially when considering politics in the developing world (Cammack *et al.*, 1993). The problems with subjective evaluations of what is democratic and what is not are highlighted by the recent proliferation of "democracies with adjectives." The emergence of countless numbers of such scholarly categorization is testament to problems associated with conceptualization (Diamond, 1996; Collier and Levitsky, 1997). According to Collier and Levitsky (1997: 440) definitions of democracy move either up or down a "ladder of generality," away from a minimum definition where hybridized democracies acquire terms such as "limited democracy," "tutelary democracy," "hard democracy," etc. As they noted, even the paradoxical label "authoritarian democracy" has appeared in the recent literature. I do not propose to test all possible types of democracies, but generally aggregate along the consensual–majoritarian dimension, relating theoretical questions on democracy and development to the issue of these qualitative aspects of democracy. I then derive hypotheses about these relationships and test them empirically.

Collusive elite?

The arguments as to why democracy, or dictatorship, promotes economic growth hinge on issues of property rights, institutional strength, investment versus consumption, and the degree to which rent-seeking activity prevails (North, 1990; Bardhan, 1993; Olson, 1993; Weede, 1996a).[11] The rent-seeking perspective is particularly dominant. Olson's (1965, 1982) earlier work identified rent seeking by collusive political and economic elites as the major determinant of why democracies experience lower growth compared to dictatorships.[12] According to the "logic of collective action," economic growth is circumscribed by collective action problems that stifle a competitive market system. Olson (1982) argued that democracies are especially prone to rent-seeking behavior and suffer from growth retarding "social rigidities" and "institutional sclerosis," which affect the efficiency of the market.

According to Olson, collective action for obtaining economic growth is difficult to achieve because rational actors are prone to free ride. Thus, even though a public good is desired by the collectivity, it might not be attainable because of the pervasiveness of free-riding activity, which requires coercion to be corrected (Olson, 1965). He argued that since the larger the entity the harder it is to insure compliance, smaller, well-organized groups are at an advantage for gaining at the expense of the larger collectivity. Given the logic of collective action, Olson (1982) posited that "distributional coalitions" form in democratic societies to gain from the fruits of state (governmental) power. The formation of these "parasitic" groups harms the welfare of the larger collectivity because of distorted markets, reduced efficiency, a crowded political agenda, hostility to new technology and reform that threatens rent seekers; in other words, the perpetuation of ineffective governance and economic stagnation. Indeed, Olson pointed out that it was war, revolution, and dictatorship that destroyed the then existing social rigidities within states, such as Germany, France, and in Japan and made possible the astounding growth performances in these countries in the postwar decades. In contrast, what was seen at the time as the "British disease" was attributed to rent seeking by distributional coalitions that managed to survive and consolidate their positions after World War II.

Governments, or the political coalitions in charge of state power, are part of the problem of rent seeking. Democratic governments in particular are thought to have a strong incentive to coalesce with effective special interest groups in the hope of benefiting from the electoral advantages that well-organized groups provide. Indeed, according to Tullock (1980: 211) "one of the major activities of modern governments is the granting of special privileges to various groups of politically influential people." Moreover, contrary to those who view democratic politics as conducive to open markets, others have shown how governments indeed "sell" protection (Grossman and Helpman, 1992). The essence of these arguments taken together suggests the "ineffectiveness" of democracies because of the strong incentives that electoral politics provide for patronage and redistribution. The larger electorate is incapable of acting as a counterweight against such activity in the center because of informational asymmetries and because the logic of collective action works powerfully against such a collective effort. Moreover, in modern representative democracies an agent represents the interests of large groups, but the agent wields institutional advantages far greater than the principal once elected to office.

What is not entirely clear from this line of reasoning, however, is the degree to which democracies are more prone to rent-seeking behavior than autocracies. In fact, Olson (1982) specified that some forms of distributional coalitions; namely, what he termed groups with "encompassing interests," would be less harmful than more narrowly based groups. Groups with encompassing interests are those that aggregate a plethora of interests to the extent that the aggregate approximates the general interest. In this way, the interests of a much broader segment of society are represented. Using this logic, Olson (1982) posited that, within democracies, two-party systems with winner-take-all electoral laws (majoritarian systems) are less likely to succumb to the vagaries of rent seeking because two-party systems are likelier to aggregate a majority of interests, approximating the general societal interest. Curiously, Olson's thesis purported to explain the "British disease," despite the fact that Britain has the prototypical majoritarian, two-party system in contrast with the successful continental states such as Germany and Italy, which have distinctively multiparty systems, sometimes called "consensual democracies."

Olson's views on democracy and development changed in later years when he argued that economic actors within democracies were bound to have longer time-horizons. Since democracies contained regularized systems of succession, they tended to increase time-horizons, whereas in a dictatorship, people would not have credible commitments as to the policies of the successor. Moreover, under dictators, people would expect succession crises, which will also work towards deterring long-term investment. Despite Olson's (1982) earlier, decidedly pessimistic outlook on democracy and economic development, his more recent expositions suggest that certain clearly specified attributes of democratic government may indeed make it less susceptible to rent-seeking behavior (Olson, 1993, 1996).

According to Olson, even though an autocrat has an encompassing interest in society, individuals do not have many guarantees that this state of affairs will always be so. Indeed, investment could very well be thwarted by a lack of guarantees coupled with the unmitigated coercive power of an autocrat. Yet, for Olson (1993: 572), even though most democracies may have shorter time-horizons than autocracies, losing a great deal of efficiency, in the "secure democracy with predictable succession of power under the rule of law, the adjudication and enforcement of individual rights are not similarly shortsighted." Once again, the arguments presented above suggest that democratic quality (its "secureness" and the extent to which the rule of law prevails) seems to matter. Not all democracies are the same!

Olson (1996) argued that democratic politics may indeed be "better" than autocracies because of the greater "efficiency" that the democratic bargaining process promotes; that is, in Olson's words, "the big bills on the sidewalk" are sure to be picked up if processes are competitive. In other words, competitive politics insures efficient markets, and markets allocate resources more efficiently than the plan, where in fact "big bills were left on the sidewalk." This line of reasoning is similar to Wittman's (1995) spirited defense of democratic efficiency. He argued that even if there were principal agent problems hampering electoral control over public officials, the competition for public office allows agents to moderate themselves. The competition and bargaining at the center among contestants for political power will insure that the majority of preferences are obtained, whether individual voters know it or not. This efficiency he attributed to institutions and the way in which policy is derived. Olson, however, never specified what exactly constitutes "secure democracy." Is it long-lasting democracy or one that simply functions better? If it is the former, then are they not the democracies he suggested suffer from "institutional sclerosis"? If they are the latter, then what makes them function better? Do all democracies insure similar degrees of competitiveness and thereby efficiency?

Detractors of Olson's pessimism about democracy argued that he fails to account for the effects of political competition as a mitigating factor on rent seeking and on efficiency, since democratic competition should not be viewed as a one-time game but as a continuous game (Wittman, 1995). Indeed, in opposition to Olson's earlier, somewhat contradictory position about the effectiveness of two-party systems, some argued that majoritarian systems, such as the Westminster system, do not necessarily aggregate the majority views more effectively than the more consensual, multiparty systems as exemplified by democracies in continental Europe (Lijphart, 1993; Crepaz, 1996; Lijphart, 1999). The US, although a two-party system, is spared some of the majoritarian problems because of federalism, judicial review, bicameralism, and the committee system, which enforce some degree of consensus and allow minority influence over the policy process.

According to these critics of Olson's arguments about "encompassing interests," majority parties in Britain and the United States are not encompassing if encompassing means that the government truly represents the majority of citizens. Many governments in majoritarian systems often do not receive a majority of votes, nor is the system conducive to meaningful competition, because a large segment of the population is left out of the policymaking arena and directly out of government (Powell, 2000). In the case of Britain, no governing party has ever obtained a majority of the votes since 1935. In fact, the governing parties in Britain have merely commanded the majority of seats in Parliament, an artifact of the electoral system that has consistently allocated seats in quite a disproportionate manner to the actual proportion of the vote received. This point is also true of the US congressional and presidential elections. The problem is exacerbated even more when only one-half of eligible voters actually go to the polls, a symptom attributable to the lack of choice and voter mobilization due, as these critics argue, to an uncompetitive party system, which constrains choice and thereby the degree of real representation in public bodies and the policy arena.

Since a simple plurality determines a party's ability to control government, it is argued that electoral politics in majoritarian systems create what might be called "electoral autocrats", albeit for limited terms. This is especially true for the pure Westminster system as it functions in Britain rather than the intricate system of separation of powers prevalent in the United States. In other words, a British government that controls Parliament without even having obtained a majority of the votes could dominate the legislative agenda because of parliamentary sovereignty, in essence a sovereignty granted to a minority, even if for a limited period of time. Thus, Lijphart (1984, 1993, 1999) and others have consistently argued that the corrective to the vote–seat mismatch and the uncompetitive nature of such a system must be the adoption of proportional representation (PR) as an electoral system, which promotes multiparty government, something that should yield dividends particularly in divided societies in poor countries where ethnic dominance is likely to bring political and economic instability. By necessitating coalitional-type arrangements, PR systems are likely to force consensus and power-sharing systems that may avoid problems associated with some groups ending up as "permanent oppositions." Importantly, however, such systems are likelier to "encompass" a broader array of opinion in the policymaking arena and prevent a seesaw of government change that may make policy unstable. Electoral systems are therefore instruments of democracy that result in democracy being qualitatively different in terms of output and the extent to which they reflect normative values associated with democracy in practice.

According to those who espouse proportionality, PR electoral systems encourage multiparty systems, which necessitate coalition governments. These systems are deemed to be more competitive since they make it very difficult for any one party to garner an absolute majority of votes and dominate the policy process. The resultant coalition building and bargaining lead to a more consensual policy environment, since coalitional partners could switch and new majorities could form to oust a winning majority. Winning majorities, thus, are likely to be more responsible in their dealings, relying on consultation, etc. Such arrangements are generally viewed as more competitive, and the governing process as more consensual.

Moreover, multiparty systems offer more choice, aggregating more interests where it counts—in the center.[13] Multipartyism also represents minority interests better and insures minority participation in government, perhaps stemming political uncertainty about the loyalties of minorities and avoiding political instability. As some have argued, liberal democracy is not just about constraining power and protecting property rights, but its practice itself can bring positive externalities. Consider Benedict Spinoza's admonition, cited in Holmes (1995: 178): "Men's natural abilities are too dull to see through everything at once; but by consulting, listening and debating, they grow more acute . . . they at last discover what they want, which all approve, but no one would have thought of in the first place."

As Lijphart (1999) demonstrates, a consensual, corporatist approach to interest aggregation and governance leads to better socioeconomic outcomes among the 36 democracies he examines. Lijphart's operationalization of the two distinct patterns of democracy as consensual and majoritarian follows the logic of several arguments within the institutional analysis framework, which see the idea of multiple veto points as necessary for safeguarding guarantees of life, liberty, and property and thus for affecting economic growth (Weingast, 1997; Henisz, 2000).[14] These arguments go somewhat beyond the narrow confines of institutional quality to connect the practice of democracy to normative values about democracy, in terms of meaningful participation and influence over policymaking and oversight of public officials.

The discussion above suggests that there is more to democracy than meets the eye, especially when it comes to determining the degree to which rent seeking can prevail, the nature of decisionmaking, and the extent to which institutions are secure. As Wittman (1995) argued, democratic bargaining works on the basis of the transitivity of preferences where the process of bargaining itself insures that the greatest number of preferences is satisfied. Since the process of democratic bargaining is not a one-time game, individual politicians and political coalitions have a strong incentive "to do the right thing." It may very well be that highly competitive democratic structures mitigate the harmful logic of collective action because high competition leads to greater oversight and transparency, serves to minimize free riding and shirking, plays an informational role, and allows a plurality of voices in the center of the political process. In this way, the optimal policy outcome is insured. In subsequent sections, I examine the notion of "secure" democracy more closely, which is crucial if democratic quality is to be satisfactorily operationalized and tested empirically.

Convulsive mass?

A crucial question about democracy, which is salient to how it relates to economic and social outcomes, is based on what Alexis de Tocqueville noted as the "two opinions which are as old as the world . . . the one tending to limit, the other to extend indefinitely, the power of the people" (cited in Powell, 2000: 3). These two opinions are embodied in two contemporary visions of democracy: the majoritarian vision that sees majority opinion vested with a powerful mandate to govern, and the proportional vision that seeks to limit majority opinion in a way that minority opinion is also reflected in democratic policymaking. If democracy is to be normatively meaningful and democratic, with policymaking reflecting the wishes of people, then democratic governance is the degree to which the people are continually able to influence policymaking, beyond the dominant interests of a simple majority. As some scholars demonstrate, institutional design based on instruments of democracy, such as elections and constitutional rules, can fashion the degree to which democratic policymaking reflects the wishes and desires of people in terms of how accessible and representative policymaking bodies become in practice (Lijphart, 1999; Powell, 2000).

As the discussion in the previous section suggests, certain types of democracies (those deemed to be "secure") may promote economic development because of the guarantees institutions provide. In Huntington's (1968) classic treatment of the crisis of politics within developing societies, he argued that it was naïve to expect a smooth transformation from traditional to modern, as modernization theories expected. He argued that the crises of governability within developing countries could be attributable to institutional incapacity. He saw institutions as being weak for handling modernizing masses that were incoherently mobilized. While old institutions were dying off, new ones had not yet been devised for effectively handling the variegated demands of a modernizing society. As Huntington (1968: 5) observed:

> equality of political participation is growing much more rapidly than the art of associating together. Social and economic change—urbanization, increases in literacy and education, industrialization, mass media expansion—extend political consciousness, multiply political demands, broaden political participation. These changes . . . enormously complicate the problem of creating new bases of political association and new political institutions combining legitimacy and effectiveness.

Low levels of institutionalization of political institutions, such as political parties, bureaucracies, and other bases of political authority, hampered consensus building and the orderly processes of governance. Even though individuals within these societies were becoming modern, political behavior was alienated and anomic, leading to heightened group consciousness, violence, clientelistic patterns of politics, increasing corruption, and the general absence of agreement on public purposes, all of which hampered effective policymaking and threatened democracy.

Huntington (1968: 78–92) offered a schema for distinguishing when mass participation is "good" and when it is "bad." He proposed that high participation with low institutionalization is likely to result in instability, whereas high participation with high levels of institutionalization resembles the character of mature democracies, where "the art of association" has been institutionalized. However, at lower levels of political institutionalization, it is also apparently propitious to keep the level of participation low. According to Huntington (1968: 70): "political systems with low levels of institutionalization and high levels of participation are systems where social forces using their own methods act directly in the political sphere." He called these "praetorian" polities. Conversely, he termed systems where institutionalization is higher relative to the level of participation "civic" polities (see Figure 4.1).

Praetorian polities are characterized by systems where the elite are accessible to the masses and where masses are available for mobilization by the elite. Praetorian politics, according to Rapoport (cited in Huntington, 1968: 80), is where "private ambitions are rarely restrained by a sense of public authority; [and] the role of power (i.e. wealth and force) is maximized." The praetorian polity is characterized as being highly unstable, even if there is absence of violence. According to Huntington (1968: 87), "In the mass (praetorian) society, political participation in unstructured, inconstant, anomic and variegated. Each social force aims to secure its objective through the resources and tactics in which it is strongest. Apathy and indignation succeed each other: the twin children of the absence of authoritative political symbols and institutions." The civic polity on the other hand displays structured participation, with political institutions that rationalize state power. The degree of participation does not affect the civic polity because of high institutionalization, which has helped to socialize the

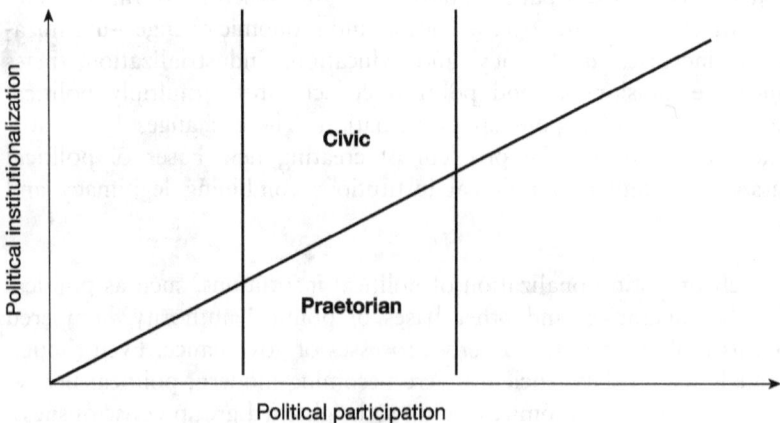

Figure 4.1 Samuel Huntington's civic versus praetorian polities. (This figure is adapted fom Huntington (1968: 79))

masses in regular political processes. Highly institutionalized political parties, for example, give coherence to voice. These arguments suggest further that there is more to "democracy" than meets the eye. Huntington's useful characterization of participant polities as being both praetorian and civic matches closely Dahl's typology of democracy as "polyarchy" (discussed below). These schemata allow us to distinguish between "good" and "bad" democracy and get closer to the ideal type of democratic governance, which has been difficult to obtain among many states in developing countries, even if they acquired all the formal trappings of democracy from colonial "masters." I explore below how I understand the concept of "democracy," a concept rarely discussed with any depth in the literature on democracy and development.

Discerning "good" democracy from "bad": a synthesis

The term "democracy" usually means many things to many people (Dahl, 2000). For example, the Soviets often eulogized their system as being more "democratic" and flaunted the notion that the ruling party was of "the people" (dictatorship of the proletariat). Soviet communists viewed Western, liberal democracy as "bourgeois democracy," or as serving only the interests of a ruling class.[15] The problem of who governs has been at the heart of democratic theory for centuries. The recent view of what democracy should mean finds its roots largely in Joseph Schumpeter's definition. Schumpeter (1943) challenged the "classical doctrine" of democracy as government whereby the majority preference obtains. According to Schumpeter, often the majority is apathetic and ignorant. He wrote that "the electoral mass is incapable of action other than a stampede" (1943: 283). He offered what is by now the most accepted conception for thinking about democracy: "That institutional arrangement for arriving at political decisions in which individuals acquire the power to decide by means of a competitive struggle for the people's vote."

In Schumpeter's view, there is little participation of the electoral mass directly in government. It is his conception of democracy as a system marked by the "competitive struggle" of a political leadership that influenced subsequent definitions of modern democracy. Robert Dahl's (1971) characterization of democracy as "polyarchy" is one of the most influential contemporary definitions of the nature of modern democratic government. Dahl argued that perfect democracy is impossible because conceptually it means the government by the masses of citizens directly, a system akin to that which existed in ancient Athens. This option, however, is a practical impossibility in large complex societies where democracy is practiced through representation. In other words, people appoint their governors successively for limited periods of time. Polyarchy, thus, is the system exhibiting the greatest degree of competitiveness when the seats of government are parceled out, and one that is most inclusive in terms of who is able to decide among the individuals and factions competing for the right to govern (see Figure 4.2).

In essence, Dahl's model is a "governance model," which captures variation in the rules that govern the governors (Lane and Ersson, 1994: 153). Dahl distinguished between closed hegemonies (no participation or contestation), inclusive hegemonies (high participation, low contestation), competitive oligarchies (high contestation, low participation) and polyarchies (both highly competitive and inclusive). The definition of democracy as "polyarchy" goes a long way to separate those systems that have high contestation from systems such as "people's democracies" and other one-party states and "ethnic hegemonies" common in the developing world, which exhibit varying degrees of contestation and participation (Weiner and Huntington, 1987). Moreover, Dahl argued that a system in which high competition preceded high inclusiveness is liable to be more stable, a sequence via which most of the "first wave" democracies appeared. To a large extent, the opposite sequence is what the "second wave" democracies experienced in the immediate postwar era when universal suffrage was regarded as *the* pillar of democratic government. Ironically, Dahl's argument rested on the assumption that polyarchy is threatened by the "demos" under conditions of highly liberalized participation. These assertions are reminiscent of Huntington's observations about praetorian and civic polities discussed above. Notice that the institutionalized (civic) polities in Huntington's graph (Figure 4.1) and those polities that are polyarchies or near-polyarchies (Figure 4.2) correspond. The same is true along the x-axis where praetorian polities can be highly inclusive (Schumpeter's "ignorant mass"), but be restrictive in terms of the level of contestation. Thus, Dahl's governance model of democracy and Huntington's schema for under-

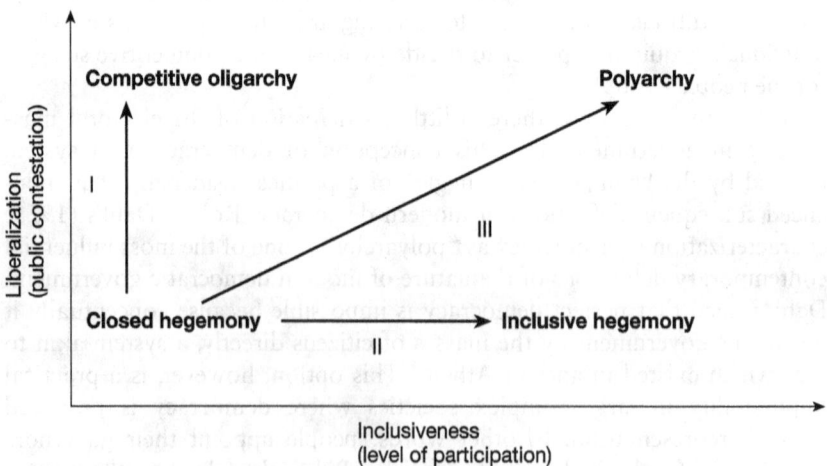

Figure 4.2 Robert Dahl's dimensions of polyarchy. (This figure is adapted from Dahl (1971: 7))

standing low and high institutionalization of democracy follow a similar logic.

The bias against mass participation in democratic theory is also reflected in the basic Hobbesian and Lockean views that preoccupied the constitution-makers in the United States. The debates during the Constitutional Congress in Philadelphia demonstrate that the impetus for formalizing the guarantees of "life, liberty, and property" in a new constitution was the threat posed to property by radical democracy. Indeed, the Constitutional Congress was convened to address the problem of radical democracy arising out of Shay's rebellion in Massachusetts and similar movements. The intricate set of checks and balances inherent in the US constitution is evidence of the concerns among many for balancing the power of all potential monopolizers of it, even against the power that democracy affords "the people." According to James Madison, writing in the Federalist Papers, "ambition must be made to counter ambition" (quoted in Wittman, 1995: 124). In other words, democracy must be "self-restraining."

There is a long history of a bias against full liberalization of political participation because of the view that political equality will somehow be a threat to economic liberty (Dahl, 1985). Such social and political observers as Alexis de Toqueville, Karl Marx, David Ricardo, and Thomas Macaulay among others recognized a permanent animus between those who controlled property and those who did not. Macaulay argued that universal suffrage would lead to "the end of property and thus of all civilization." Ricardo wrote that the use of the vote should only be the prerogative of "that part of them which cannot be supposed to have an interest in overturning the right to property" (quoted in Przeworski and Limongi, 1993: 53). It was such rationalizations that prompted property requirements for the right to vote in both the US and Britain. According to Seymour Martin Lipset (Lipset, 1959: 75):

> From Aristotle down to the present, men have argued that only in a wealthy society in which relatively few citizens lived in real poverty could a situation exist in which the mass of the population could intelligently participate in politics and could develop the self restraint necessary to avoid succumbing to the appeals of irresponsible demagogues.

Theorists of democracy, therefore, have always been wary of the "demos." As many argue, the success of Western democracy is largely a function of gradual liberalization of participation characterized by the pattern followed by Western and Northern Europe and North America. This pattern of liberalization of participation, however, was unavailable to the newly decolonized "second wave" democracies, which adopted (or in many instances were forced to adopt) fully liberalized polities on the same lines as those of the metropole (Dahl, 1971; Dix, 1994).[16] This point holds especially true for the "third wave" democracies emerging from behind the iron curtain, which for historic reasons especially, have already adopted universal suffrage as a matter of course.[17]

Recognizing the dangers of radical democracy, nevertheless, Dahl argued that "polyarchy" is best served by a competitive system that regularizes the norms and rules of politics long before mass participation is allowed. These polities also foster a political culture of "deference" (reminiscent of conditions favorable for the developmental state), which allows these systems some insulation from the vagaries of mass politics, giving state institutions a reasonable amount of autonomy. The failure of many of the "second wave" democracies that appeared after decolonization in the postwar era is explained precisely and fundamentally as resulting from "crises of governability" under conditions of mass politics (Binder, 1971). It is precisely in this vein that some warned against the optimism of early modernization theories and highlighted that the failure of democracy and development stemmed from the institutional incapacity of states to handle the political demands and pressures of societal groups acting en masse (Huntington, 1968; Nelson, 1987; Weiner and Huntington, 1987). Huntington and Nelson (1976: 19) put it bluntly—"participation must be held down, at least temporarily, in order to promote economic development." The question of governability and economic performance corresponds in a general sense with transaction cost arguments. Some democratic constitutional arrangements may not be conducive to what is sometimes referred to as "market-preserving federalism" (Weingast, 1993).

One major aspect of how democracies are supposedly less susceptible to rent seeking, thereby exhibiting more efficiency, is argued on the basis of the principal–agent relationship. Unlike in a dictatorship where a dictator is both principal and agent, in a democracy, the eligible voter may transmit preferences to an agent, who is in turn controlled by the principal's ability to punish by "throwing a rascal out" of office at the next election. This factor apparently induces responsible behavior on the part of the agent who acts in the interests of a broader constituency rather than using politics for private gain. However, the shortcomings of this perspective are highlighted by the principal–agent problem, whereby the agent is at a distinct advantage vis-à-vis the principal and could benefit from the huge information asymmetry between them.[18] For example, it is highly unlikely that the average voter (especially in a poor country) is likely to ever know whether or not her representative is corrupt, leave alone the everyday details about politics and policymaking. However, from the perspective of a highly contested system, it is perhaps far less costly for the principal to acquire at least adequate information, and the costs of engaging in corrupt behavior are likely to be high since the machinery of party politics should work toward making this so. In the praetorian system, on the other hand, clientelist patterns promote corruption, which often comes in the form of buying support among narrow bases of political support, and the voter is faced with choosing between two known crooks. In such settings, it is no surprise that the voter is highly cynical and violence highly likely (Huntington, 1968). Consider the dilemma of the Pakistani voter, who has come to accept even military rule because of corrupt democratic governance.

In the postwar years, in the developing world especially, democracy had little chance of surviving when multiethnic states struggled simultaneously to define the nation, create growth and equity, and satisfy the strident demands of competing groups. Thus, one other causal link between high competition and economic development might be that competitive politics, as it has been argued generally about democracy, acts as insurance against ethnic monopolization, prevents massive polarization resulting from possible violence, and thus, reinforces the relative "safety" of "life, liberty, and property" under conditions of polarized interests. In other words, high degrees of competition guarantee that no one monopolizes power to the detriment of others.[19] North (1990: 53) explained these relationships in terms of political efficiency leading to economic efficiency. The vote is one way in which the power of government, or entrenched groups, is diffused throughout society, minimizing the possibility of arbitrary rule or parasitic behavior. The individual in a democratic society gains a "voice" in matters of government but voice is likely to be translated into action given stiff competition and accountability among the governors (the agents). What Huntington termed "civic" therefore can be reinterpreted to mean the degree to which the state is contestable, which offers greater security and a voice for diverse opinion and often a stake in government itself.

In general, under highly competitive systems, therefore, no one party, whether a single person or group, or the "demos" collectively in the form of people's parties, dominant ethnic parties, etc., is likely to gain enough power to be dictatorial and capricious at the expense of the rest of society—in other words, to be praetorian. Institutions that foster a more competitive political process, while having reasonably high participation, perhaps diffuse the intensities of popular pressure on state institutions. A competitive system, in Robert Putnam's (1993) view, would also reflect a greater degree of civic participation as opposed to the anomic participation that may be inherent in polities that have little contestation and interest aggregation in the center. Putnam (1993: 109) put it bluntly when he wrote, "it is not the degree of participation that distinguishes civic from uncivic regions, but its character." Like democracy, participation in political life comes in various forms and the essence of what is democratic should not be reduced to the degree to which "rights" might exist but how such rights translate into democracy in practice. The key to whether democracy matters for economic growth or not hinge, as many argue, on the way in which the system is able to build the necessary coalitional arrangement to solve collective action problems and distributive conflicts inherent in political life (Haggard, 1990; Rodrik, 1999).

The two visions of democracy that are "as old as the world"—majoritarian and proportionality—reflect the degree to which powerful "opinion" is

checked and moderated and the degree to which policymaking is representative and accessible to society at large. The empirical example of the
successful growth experience of the East Asian NICs reinforces the point on
governability under mass participation where majority opinion is allowed
to dominate. The authoritarian character of many of these states (Haggard,
1990) and the hijacking of populist democracy in many Latin American
countries, such as Chile, occurred ostensibly to thwart populist redistribution and insure efficient economic policies (O'Donnell, 1995). Such
struggles may be viewed as stemming from the lack of consensual processes,
where powerful opinion threatened minority rights, which in the case of
Latin America happened to be that of the militarily powerful, land-owning
capitalist elite. Apparently, there was no guarantee that democracies would
automatically protect property rights, because, as the Chilean experience
during the 1980s exemplified, a dictatorship under General Pinochet to
protect property rights, whereas a democratically elected leader, Salvador
Allende, tried to expropriate property. Thus, there seem to be qualitative
differences among types of "democracy" as there surely are among autocracies. How can we incorporate such variation in tests of democracy and
growth without painting all democracies the same colour, which is what
empirical analyses have done thus far? The answer may depend on how one
conceptualizes and then operationalizes democracy objectively in empirical
studies.

The hypotheses, variables, and data

I have argued that addressing the issue of democracy and growth by
looking at regime type dichotomously, where differing types of democracy
are heaped together, will result in the null result obtained in empirical
studies. Instead, looking at qualitative differences, or institutional variation, within democracies may yield better answers as to the nature of the
relationship between democracy and growth. It is also argued here that the
pessimistic outlook on democracy and growth, which is based largely on
arguments involving the threat to property because of politicization and
mass participation, and the optimistic outlook, based on arguments of the
advantages of a competitive process rather than collusion, are perhaps
both correct.

In order to test this synthesized conceptualization, I use Robert Dahl's
(1971, 1985) precise definition of democracy as polyarchy. According to
Dahl, there can be closed hegemonies (fully authoritarian), highly competitive systems, highly participatory systems, and polyarchies, which are high
on both dimensions. I distinguish "high intensity" democracies as those
that lack competition relative to participation, or those which Huntington
(1968) viewed as containing "praetorian" qualities rather than institutionalized and regularized features of democratic governance. The flip side of
this relationship is "low intensity" democracies that exhibit a high level of

political "competition" where a majority opinion will be more easily checked. The hypothesis is that democracy will exhibit positive effects on growth only if the ratio of competition to participation on Dahl's degree of polyarchy is higher than the ratio of participation to competition. In other words, I expect a greater degree of competition to promote growth, while democracy that shows little likelihood that a majority will be easily checked is likely to exhibit lower growth. This hypothesis is derived from a synthesized view of the optimists and pessimists on the issue of democracy and economic growth, and in fact the two visions of democracy discussed above.

While the hypothesis stated here is theoretically derived from discussions of the nature of democracy and how it might be related to economic development, operationalizing democracy to capture the precise definitions of the two visions of democracy is a practical one. The widely used measures of democracy in similar studies are all subjectively derived and largely do not consider the institutional variations that define objectively important variations within democracy. This study uses Tatu Vanhanen's (1990, 1992, 1993) electoral data as its primary measure of democracy. These data are objectively derived from electoral results and measure the competitiveness of the party structure and the degree of participation of the population at large in electoral competitions for state power. In essence, Vanhanen provided a measure of polyarchy in the Dahlian conception of democracy because his democracy measure is simply competition × participation expressed as a percentage (democracy = competition × participation). Although Vanhanen's data are used by many comparativists (Dix, 1994), they have not been used in any tests of the democracy and economic growth issue to date. Previous studies on democracy and economic growth have mainly used Raymond Gastil's data published as the Freedom House series, the polity index of democracy (Gurr and Jaggers, 1995), and Kenneth Bollen's (1993) measure of democracy (see Barro, 1996, 1998).

The competition component of the index of democracy essentially measures "the existence of legal competition," the degree to which "individuals and groups are free to organize themselves and to oppose the government" and "the existence of some degree of equality among the different groups competing for power." Essentially, competition is taken to be the "narrowness" by which the largest party wins a given election. Thus, the closer the percentage of the vote separating the largest party from the combined percentage received by all the parties participating in any given election, the more competitive that system is judged to be. In other words, the greater the opportunity for a coalition to form against the governing party at any given time, the more competitive is the system because the governor's powers are tenuous. Moreover, the more competitive the system, the less likely that the largest party will always dominate. Accordingly, this variable is set up to favor multiparty systems that are ostensibly more consensual and allow greater representation and accessibility in the policy process (Lijphart,

1993; Powell, 2000). Competition is measured as [100 – (largest party's percentage of vote)], or alternatively, the percentage of the vote received by all parties other than the largest. Vanhanen used a cutoff point for competition where all the smaller parties must receive at least 30 percent of the total votes cast. Gastil also applied this rule in his categorization of fair elections. In other words, if any single party consistently receives more than 70 percent of the vote, those elections are deemed to have been uncompetitive and undemocratic. The application of these strict criteria insures that elections that have most likely been rigged are disregarded.

The participation component measures the degree of participation in "crucial decision-making processes . . . [and] is indicative of the relative number of people participating in politics in general" (Vanhanen, 1992: 22). The percentage of people voting in any election is taken against the total population rather than by criteria of voter eligibility because many states have *de jure* and *de facto* eligibility criteria for discouraging participation. This method also minimizes the bias inherent in eligibility criteria that affect LDCs, where high percentages of the populations are relatively very young. There is a 15 percent threshold used by the coding rules for participation because an election that does not elicit at least a 15 percent voter turnout is suspected of being fraudulent and unrepresentative of true democracy.

I agree with Vanhanen's (1990: 23) assessment that "the two indicators based on competition and participation are the most important dimensions of democratization and that these simple quantitative indicators based on electoral data are enough to measure the major differences between political systems and their level of democratization." Moreover, I also agree that some measures of democracy, such as Gastil's and Bollen's, which primarily measure civil liberties, tend to be based on rather subjective criteria. Arguably, quantitative measures of competition and participation based on hard evidence such as electoral data reflect reality better. As Vanhanen (1990: 23) pointed out, "legal competition for power would not be possible without civil and political liberties."

Indeed, the right to contest for office, or the right to participate in elections, exists in many cases only in *de jure* terms, whether one considers "monist" party elections in many of the Latin American, African, and Southeast Asian states, or the meaningless plebiscites that were (and are still) ubiquitous in many communist/populist/religious-fundamentalist states. This study argues, therefore, that the "fact" of competition and participation is a sound measure of the extent of democracy, despite the fact that it does not explicitly take into account civil liberty. Gasiorowski (1996: 478) compared the polity data, Gastil's Freedom House data, and Vanhanen's index of democracy and found that Vanhanen's measure correlated best with his own new data set, the "Political regime change data set" for the 1980–8 period. Vanhanen's democracy score is correlated r = 0.75 with Gasiorowski's data. The polity data was second highest with

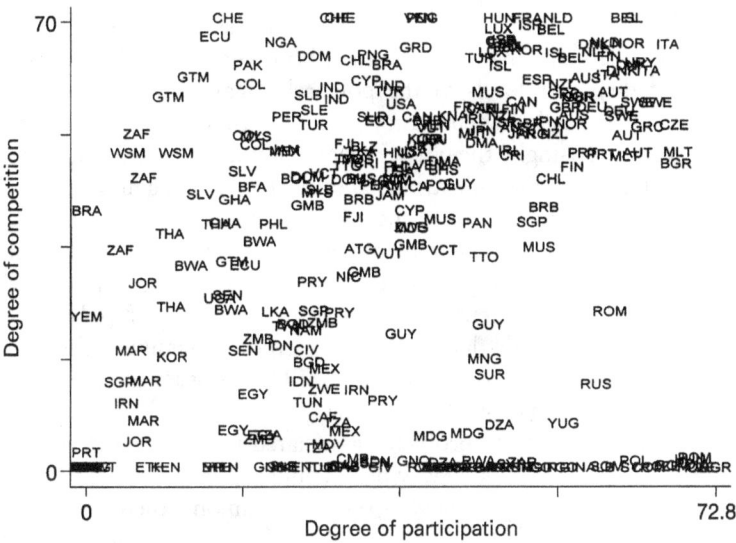

Figure 4.3 Degree of competition and participation (Vanhanen's index of democracy), 1970, 1980, 1990

r = 0.68, while the Freedom House index scored comparatively lower. Nevertheless, measures of democracy somewhat differently measured and defined do not preclude high levels of congruence among them. For three points in time (1970, 1980, and 1990) covering 390 data points, the three measures used in this study show very high congruence. The correlation between Polity IV and the Freedom House index is r = −0.89 (Freedom House is coded on a scale of 7 = most democratic, down to 1 = least democratic, hence the negative sign). The very high correlation between the two is not surprising given that these two indices are somewhat similarly derived in terms of the method of assessing. Despite the fact that Vanhanen's data only reflect voting results, however, they are highly compatible with the two subjectively derived measures. The Polity IV data and Vanhanen's index are highly correlated (r = 0.86), and Vanhanen's index and the Freedom House data are similarly highly congruent (r = −0.85).

Next, I examine the degree of variance between democracies as captured by Vanhanen's objectively derived data. What Vanhanen's data for three points in time covered by this study (1970, 1980, and 1990) show is the varying degrees of contestation and participation that result in somewhat different levels of "democracy" along the polyarchy scale. Figure 4.3 displays the degree of democracy (polyarchy) measured along the dimensions of contestation and participation for roughly 100 countries over three years, 1970, 1980, and 1990.

The graph displays the degree of competition on the y-axis and the degree of participation on the x-axis. Full polyarchies are clearly evident at the top right-hand side of the space where high contestation and high participation come together. What is interesting, however, is to see how most countries are at disparate levels of the polyarchy scale, despite having a system of government called "democracy" in the normative understanding of the term. Not surprisingly, the cluster of polyarchies is largely the older democracies that are also the industrialized ones. To view this more clearly, Figure 4.4 captures this dimension at one point in time; namely, in 1980. As seen there, it is normatively harder to discern the degree of difference in "democracy" among, for example, Nigeria (NGA), Sri Lanka (LKA), and Guyana (GUY) in 1980, except along an objective scale of polyarchy. Moreover, the polyarchy scale does not readily capture massive differences in degree of contestation among PR and SMP systems, although there seems to be a slight bias against SMP systems.

Again, the graph depicts the problems associated with assigning subjectively derived scores to democracy, where countries at similar levels of democracy may in fact simply show no variance among them, or some countries may in fact be affected one way or another given some factor of political life that may come to be overemphasized as more democratic or vice versa as a result of special events, particularly momentary news stories that are dramatic. For example, from a subjective sense, if the recent threats—perceived and real—to civil liberties in the US stemming from concerns about "homeland security" after the attacks of September 11 2001 were to have taken place in a poor third-world country, would it have withstood subjective evaluations of its "democratic status" from afar? The

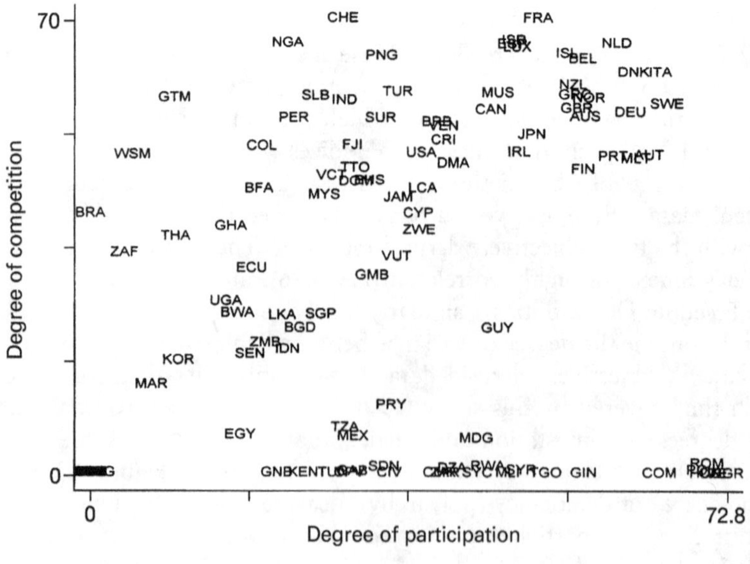

Figure 4.4 Degree of competition and participation (Vanhanen's index of democracy), 1980

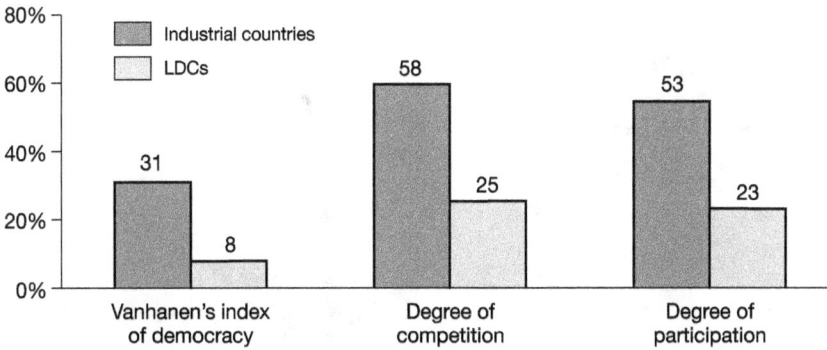

Figure 4.5 Comparison of means between rich countries (n = 53) and LDCs (n = 194), averaged over three decades (1970s, 1980s, and 1990s))

recent events in Spain are particularly illustrative. If a poor country were to ban the political party of a minority group because of suspected links to violent terrorists, would it be viewed as upholding the constitutional order and protecting innocent citizens from terror, or as ethnic hegemony and political discrimination?

Figure 4.5 presents the mean values of democracy (polyarchy), the degree of competition, and the degree of participation among the rich, industrialized countries (see Data appendix for list) and the LDCs averaged over the three points in time, 1970, 1980, and 1990.

As seen there, the mean value for polyarchy among the poor countries is just eight, while it is 31 for the rich countries, almost four times as much. Examining the Polity IV data (results not shown), one of the most widely used subjective indices, the difference among the same data points is only a factor of two, so that rich countries were only twice as "democratic" as the poor ones. The large gaps in the levels of contestation and the degree of participation are also noteworthy. This simple examination demonstrates the need both for closer examination of substantive issues about regime type and growth and for the use of alternative measures in theoretically cogent ways in our empirical assessments. It is, after all, on the solid empirical assessments obtained thus far that strong consensus on regime type and growth largely rests. The following chapter presents my results.

5 Empirics of democracy and growth, and growth of democracy

Introduction

The following analyses utilize roughly the same data and economic growth models used previously in Chapter 3 to test the relationship between foreign capital and growth. I retain the rates of investment of both foreign and domestic investment given their strong relationship with growth. Leaving foreign capital in the models also allows me to hold constant the argument that foreign investment may in fact compensate for the growth effects within autocracies, such as China and the Asian and Latin American NICs. It is only in these slight changes that my growth models are different from the standard Barro-type growth models that dominate the literature. As mentioned previously, I do not follow Barro (1998) in every respect, but replicate as closely as possible his influential analyses on this topic.

I enter the democracy variables measured at the beginning of the growth period in order to minimize the bias of simultaneity between growth and democracy. According to one prominent study on this subject, the relationship between the growth rate and democracy has been overstated (Przeworski and Limongi, 1997). This careful analysis found no evidence to suggest that higher growth rates at any point in time lead to democracy. The analysis reported, however, that it is largely true for the *level* of wealth, which of course I hold constant in all three panels.

Robert Barro's empirical analyses on endogenous growth models stand out in the literature. According to Barro (1998), it is best that the determinants of economic growth be assessed by utilizing the cross-national method, since many of the variables of interest, such as the level of human capital and democracy, show very little intertemporal variation. For example, there may be very little variation in a democracy score over time for any given country while the growth rate varies a great deal from year to year. Barro (2001) also recommended that tests of democracy on growth be conducted on average growth rates over a longer period of time because there might be a lag in time before private economic actors find reassurance in policy stability. I use the 10-year average that he employs in his studies.

Following Barro (1996, 1998) this study examines a group of panels containing roughly 97 countries for which data is available between 1970 and 1999, a span of almost three decades.[1] The 10-year averaged panel data are ideal for addressing the question at hand because I am primarily interested in the cross-national dimensions of democracy as they relate to growth. The within-country dimension is less important, since an individual country is subject to external constraints on its growth rate as growth rates are generally influenced by global business cycles and trends. Thus, what is important is given a value of democracy of country j, what it does in terms of growth relative to others in the sample over the three decades. The dependent variable is per capita economic growth rate between 1970 and 1999 in three 10-year period averages. All control variables except trade to GDP are measures at the beginning of the growth period. Trade to GDP is the average over each decade.

This study replicates Barro's (1998) model with some modification, incorporating evidence from empirical tests of the robustness of variables explaining growth as discussed in the previous chapter. I incorporate a measure of trade openness in addition to the FDI variables given the theoretical links made between democracy and trade, and democracy and free markets (Milner and Kubota, 2001). The human capital variable is described in detail in the previous chapter. Human capital is crucial when examining the effects of democracy on growth given the close association between democracy and components of human capital, such as schooling, under-five mortality, and fertility.

I also test the relationship between economic freedom, democracy, and growth. The measure of economic freedom that I use is widely recognized as a good measure of the degree to which property rights exist and is one of the longest existing of its kind (Gwartney *et al.*, 2001).[2] I test specifically whether or not democracy's relationship to growth (as conceptualized by me) is purely a function of property rights arguments, or whether democratic decisionmaking (policymaking) provides added explanation. The economic freedom index measures the degree to which private actors are allowed to participate in economic life. It measures countries on five main dimensions, which in turn consist of several subdimensions: size of government—expenditures, taxes, and enterprises—legal structure and security of property, supply of sound money, freedom to trade with foreigners, and regulation of credit, labour, and business. Each of the five areas was scored on many subcategories, totaling 39 criteria, most of which relate to purely economic concerns, particularly the extent to which rights to property effectively exist, the ways in which courts function, and corruption (see Gwartney *et al.*, 2001 for extensive description of method).

Results and conclusions

Table 5.1 contains the results of the effects of democracy and growth, where I replicate other studies using alternative measures of democracy.

Table 5.1 Alternative measures of democracy and economic growth, 1970–99

Variables	(1)	(2)	(3)	(4)
FDI investment rate	0.033[†]	0.035[†]	0.034[†]	0.036[†]
	(2.2)	(2.2)	(2.2)	(2.3)
Domestic investment	0.42[§]	0.43[§]	0.42[§]	0.43[§]
rate	(8.8)	(8.7)	(8.8)	(8.9)
Log size (GDP)	0.30[§]	0.29[§]	0.29[§]	0.27[§]
	(3.9)	(3.7)	(3.9)	(3.6)
Trade/GDP	0.008[§]	0.007[§]	0.007[†]	0.007[†]
	(2.6)	(2.6)	(2.5)	(2.4)
Log initial income/pc	−1.4[§]	−1.4[§]	−1.5[§]	−1.4[§]
	(−5.4)	(−5.5)	(−5.8)	(−5.1)
Time dummy 1970–80	0.89[§]	0.81[†]	0.90[§]	0.79[†]
	(2.7)	(2.4)	(2.7)	(2.3)
Time dummy 1980–90	−0.18	−0.18	−0.08	−0.12
	(−0.66)	(−0.65)	(−0.29)	(−0.42)
Human capital	1.2[§]	1.2[§]	1.2[§]	1.2[§]
	(7.2)	(6.7)	(6.6)	(6.9)
FDI stock/GDP	−0.004	−0.002	−0.002	−0.005
	(−0.35)	(−0.35)	(−0.26)	(−0.58)
Domestic stock/GDP	0.004[§]	0.004[§]	0.005[§]	0.005[§]
	(2.9)	(3.0)	(3.1)	(3.2)
Political rights (Gastil)	−0.035			
	−0.51			
Polity IV		0.012		
		(0.67)		
Vanhanen ID			0.017	0.040[†]
			(1.4)	(2.4)
Vanhanen				−0.017
participation				(−1.6)
Constant	4.9[†]	4.4[†]	4.8[†]	4.9[†]
	(2.5)	(2.2)	(2.5)	(2.5)
F	34.7	34.8	36.6	35.64
p-value	0.0000	0.0000	0.0000	0.0000
R^2	0.65	0.65	0.65	0.65
N	244	245	246	246
Countries	97	97	97	97

Notes
Huber-White robust standard errors computed in all tests.
*   denotes $p < 0.10$
†   denotes $p < 0.05$
§   denotes $p < 0.01$ (two-tailed)

In column 1, I enter the Freedom House index of political rights in the basic growth model. As seen there, democracy measured as political rights has no statistically significant effect on growth, findings congruent with the recent empirical consensus on the subject. While political rights have no effect on growth, it is not negative as pessimists on democracy would have it. A similar result obtains in column 2 with the Polity IV measure of democracy.[3] The control variables essentially remain the same as in the tests presented in the previous chapter on FDI and growth. Moreover, FDI's effects on growth are unaffected in the presence of democracy in the models, suggesting that FDI has independent effects on growth, holding regime type constant. These results generally mirror Barro's (1998) results except that I am unable to confirm the statistically significant curvilinear shape between democracy and growth reported by him (results not shown).

In column 3, I enter Vanhanen's index of democracy. As seen there, democracy's independent effect on growth is quite a bit more significant than the other two indicators of democracy, but it does not reach statistical significance at conventional levels. In column 4, when participation is added independently, however, the Vanhanen index of democracy gains strong statistical significance, indicating an independent effect of the competitive aspect of democracy over that of democracies high on the degree of participation. In fact, the independent effect of the degree of participation is negatively associated with growth and only just fails statistical significance at the 90 percent level. The two terms are jointly significant, however, at the 95 percent level (F [2, 96] = 2.9, p < 0.05). Substantively, a percentage increase in democracy increases growth by 0.04 percent, but a percentage increase in democracy contextually is meaningless, since a country moving from 0 to 1 percent is still 99 percent authoritarian. A more pleasing substantive interpretation is to suppose that if a country moves from the mean value of LDC democracies (8) to that of the industrialized countries (31), which is a 23-percentage-point increase, a poor country adds almost 1 percent to its growth rate. This added benefit to developing countries net of the other variables in the model is not insignificant considering that many poor countries had negative growth rates during these three decades.

These results are tentative support for the main hypothesis propounded by this study based on theoretical arguments over what is good about democracy on the issue of growth. If democracy is competitive so that it is able to check majority "opinion," then such features of democracy matter positively for growth. On the other hand, the data show that democracy that loosely reflects majoritarian tendencies suffers lower growth. It seems as if the participation component of democracy is detrimental to growth, controlling for the degree of competition. The results support the notion that institutional variation in terms of how politics is structured within democracy matters and that the size of the "selectorate" matters less than the size of the "ruling coalition" in terms of the way in which it may reflect

Table 5.2 Democracy, economic freedom, and economic growth, 1970–99

Variables	(1)	(2)	(3)	(4)
FDI investment rate	0.035†	0.035†	0.078§	0.077§
	(2.4)	(2.4)	(6.0)	(5.7)
Domestic investment rate	0.41§	0.41§	0.43§	0.42§
	(8.8)	(8.7)	(8.3)	(8.1)
Log size (GDP)	0.30§	0.30§	0.28§	0.30§
	(4.1)	(4.0)	(3.3)	(3.6)
Trade/GDP	0.007†	0.007†	0.002	0.003
	(2.4)	(2.5)	(0.77)	(1.1)
Log initial income/pc	−1.4§	−1.4§	−1.2§	−1.4§
	(−5.2)	(−5.6)	(−3.8)	(−4.4)
Time dummy 1970–80	0.92§	0.89†	0.45	0.39
	(2.7)	(2.6)	(1.3)	(1.1)
Time dummy 1980–90	−0.06	−0.09	−0.36	−0.27
	(−0.21)	(−0.32)	(−1.3)	(−0.99)
Human capital	1.2§	1.2§	1.2§	1.1§
	(6.3)	(6.1)	(6.9)	(5.5)
FDI stock/GDP	−0.003	−0.004	0.018†	0.017*
	(−0.48)	(−0.66)	(2.0)	(1.8)
Domestic stock/GDP	0.004§	0.004§	0.002	0.001
	(2.8)	(2.7)	(1.2)	(1.1)
Vanhanen ID	0.047§	−0.030		−0.041
	(2.6)	(−0.69)		(−1.0)
Vanhanen participation	−0.016	0.040*		0.044†
	(−1.5)	(1.7)		(2.1)
LDC dummy	0.62*	1.2*	0.25	0.76
	(1.8)	(1.7)	(0.65)	(1.0)
LDC dummy × Vanhanen ID		0.080*		0.084*
		(1.7)		(1.8)
LDC dummy × participation		−0.060†		−0.055†
		(2.2)		(−2.2)
Economic freedom			−0.065	−0.018
			(−0.75)	(−0.14)
Constant	4.1†	3.5	4.2†	4.2*
	(2.0)	(1.5)	(2.0)	(1.9)
F	35.8	31.3	31.3	29.9
p-value	0.0000	0.0000	0.0000	0.0000
R^2	0.66	0.66	0.71	0.72
N	246	246	209	209
Countries	97	97	89	89

Notes
Huber-White robust standard errors computed in all tests.
* denotes $p < 0.10$
† denotes $p < 0.05$
§ denotes $p < 0.01$ (two-tailed)

interests. However, it may be argued that the negative effect of higher levels of participation may indeed be coming from a residual convergence effect, since rich, democratic countries also sport the highest levels of electoral participation.[4] I test this proposition next by adding a dummy variable for LDCs defined as countries that are not industrialized democracies. The definition for industrialized democracies is the same as that for the "core" countries as operationalized in the tests on FDI and growth (Western European, North American, Australasian democracies, plus Japan).

In Table 5.2, column 1, I enter a dummy variable for developing countries (LDCs) which takes on the value 1 for each LDC but 0 for the rich countries.

As seen there, the LDC effect is positive and statistically significant despite the fact that initial wealth is also included in the model. Given that many very rich, oil wealthy countries have also been growing very slowly, this result is not all that surprising. This result perhaps also accounts for the curvilinear shape in Barro's (1998) analyses, where very high levels of democracy, as reflected in the data for the old democracies, suffer residual convergence effects, which are not accounted for stringently enough in his models. However, what is interesting for me is to compute the exact effects of my measures of democracy among the developing countries, since many of the rich, industrialized countries, normatively at least according to some, have concerns driven by postmodernist values that are unsupportive of growth (Granato *et al.*, 1996).

In Table 5.2 column 2, I enter the interactive term of the LDC dummy and Vanhanen's index of democracy (LDC dummy × Vanhanen ID), and the product of the LDC dummy and participation (LDC dummy × participation). As seen there, democracy among the LDCs predicts growth positively, a result highly unlikely to have been obtained by chance. The degree of participation among the LDCs is strongly negative, holding the degree of competitiveness constant.[5] Notice that the opposite effect is true for the industrialized democracies. The level of democracy is weakly negatively related to growth while the level of participation has a positive (statistically significant) effect on the rate of per capita economic growth. Apparently, among the developed countries, it is higher levels of participation that are positively associated with growth, holding the degree of competition constant. Tentatively, these results support others which find that older democracies may suffer from "institutional sclerosis" and thereby lower growth (Lane and Ersson, 1986). However, there is also clear support for Lijphart's arguments that call for increasing participation in the electorates within developed democracies for ensuring even more competition at the center. Since competition requires participation—that is, participation is endogenous to competition and the differences among the established democracies are small—it might very well be that higher competition's nonsignificant effect on growth among the rich countries reflects the ability of smaller parties, such as the Greens, to affect policy with postmodern concerns that are inimical to growth. Yet again, the result may suggest that those rich countries that are distinctively majoritarian, such as the UK, US, Australia, and New Zealand, have performed better than the proportional democracies for reasons other than those which affect growth in the opposite direction in poor countries. The reasons for these small differences among the rich countries may be many and warrant closer examination in future research.

The major issue, however, remains that the two components of democracy have a different effect on growth (affecting poor and rich countries somewhat differently), effects which are statistically significant. It is clear that in terms of the issue of regime type and growth not all democracies have similar effects on output—democratic structure matters. These results suggest that the inconclusive nature of accumulated research on this topic is largely a function of how democracy is conceptualized, measured, and tested. These empirical results support those who argue that institutional variation, rather than regime type, is what is important for growth. In other words, the quality of democracy matters for governance-related outcomes.

What do these statistically significant results actually mean substantively? Since the democracy index in the Vanhanen scheme is an interactive term between the level of competition and the level of participation, the test presented in column 2 of Table 5.2 can be rerun including an interactive term of competition among the LDCs, which allows us to interpret the substantive effects of these two components of polyarchy separately for a given increase in their values (results not shown). Taking the parameter estimates of the interactive term of the dummy variable for democracy among the LDCs with its component parts (competition and participation) included, we get a parameter estimate of 0.04 for index of democracy, −0.04 for participation, and 0.02 for competition (joint significance = $p < 0.01$). We can now compute the independent effects of each component, holding the other at its mean value (see Data appendix for summary statistics).

Holding the level of competition among all LDCs at its mean value (36), a percentage increase in participation can decrease the growth rate by 0.04 (36/100) + the parameter estimate of participation (−0.04), which equals −0.026 percent. Likewise, a percentage increase in the level of competition holding participation at its mean (33) can increase growth by 0.033 percent. This means that in the real world, a country that moves from dictatorship (0) to being a competitive polity similar to an industrial democracy (50 percent) can increase its growth rate by 1.7 percent per annum (with participation at the LDC mean of 33 percent). On the other hand, holding competition at the LDC mean (38), a country that raises its level of participation by 50 percentage points risks lowering its annual average growth rate by 1.2 percent.[6] These effects are significant given that the mean annual average growth rate among the LDCs over the three decades is 1.1 percent. However, holding participation at the mean value and increasing the degree of competition necessarily mean increasing democracy conceptualized as the degree of competition, since participation is endogenous to competition. The substantive effects are net of the effects of all the other variables in the model, suggesting that democracy's contribution is not something to be ignored.

Democracy does seem to have a substantial direct effect on growth, given the values of the control variables, but these results depend heavily on gauging institutional variation within democracies. Good democracies are not ones that just have inclusive participation; they must also offer choice at the center, check arbitrary and lopsided policymaking, and insure consensual decisionmaking by being truly competitive. I leave it to future research to tease out exactly which one of these factors associated with the two visions of democracy is most important for growth. For the moment, however, the assumption that they all work in tandem to promote efficient government compared to autocracies is a safe one.

To understand clearly whether or not it is democracy's structure or the quality of institutions based on respect for property rights and the prevalence of economic freedom, I add "economic freedom" to the model without the democracy variables in Table 5.2, column 3. As seen there, economic freedom is negative and statistically not different from zero. Subjective evaluations of economic freedom do not predict growth above the variables measuring trade, FDI, human capital, and the size of the domestic market. Interestingly, all variables remain the same except that trade to GDP is now statistically not significant and the "penetration of FDI" (FDI stock/GDP) is positive and significant on growth. It seems that the nonsignificant effect of the influence of FDI in an economy for growth reported in the previous chapter is dependent on the exclusion of some cases, since the inclusion of economic freedom reduces the sample size by 40. The result does not seem to be driven by any connection between economic freedom and FDI because running the model without economic freedom but excluding the same cases yields a similar result.[7] In column 4, including the democracy measures with economic freedom barely changes the previous results on democracy and growth. It seems that the political variables are robust to specification and sample size and significant for growth independently of economic freedom. Perhaps the variables measuring openness to trade and FDI capture economic freedom adequately enough.

These findings show why it is true that some autocracies fared better than some democracies in achieving economic growth. While many have alluded to this point, it had never been demonstrated empirically, nor explained theoretically (Alesina *et al.*, 1992; Barro, 1998). As the modernization literature has suggested, authoritarianism in many parts of the world arose in response largely to the problems of mass participation and the resultant instabilities following decolonization. The negative coefficient for highly participatory democracy, a result that is consistent and robust, supports the position that high participation, holding competitiveness of the party structure constant, is indeed inimical to economic growth. Does this paradoxical result warrant the degree of pessimism regarding democracy and economic growth that is generally reflected in the modernization literature on political development à la Samuel Huntington? I suggest not.

At first glance, the negative effects of participation on growth are troubling because participation is, after all, one crucial pillar of democracy. However, the degree of participation is endogenous to both competition and democracy (there cannot be competition without participation). Therefore, it is the lack of democracy defined as the degree of contestation that suppresses growth. As the comparison of means tests above illustrates, LDCs as a group comparative to the industrialized countries show far poorer scores on this dimension of democracy than on the degree of participation. Since the degree of contestation is connected to the ways in which democracy aggregates preferences and reflects the degree of representativeness of social divisions within the policy process, these results show that such processes matter positively for growth. Clearly, since participation has a growth lowering tendency, controlling for competition, it seems to be that it is the populist, politicized, aspects of democracy that make it incompatible with economic growth, where majority opinion can seesaw between growth promoting and redistributive tendencies, an outcome that is apparent in many poor countries characterized by high policy instability. Indeed, designing institutions to enhance contestation through electoral systems and other mechanisms is a good option for making democracy more representative, consensual, stable, and responsive (Lijphart, 1999; Powell, 2000). Democratic design has an impact on economic growth, as it surely does for affecting other outcomes such as social stability.

At the time of decolonization of many LDCs, the majoritarian vision, even if institutions did not reflect such a tendency, was seen as desirable for nation-building, forging identity, reducing societal demands and conflicts, and cushioning the state elite to "plan" development. What happened often within LDCs in the postwar era was that politicization triggered the abandonment of democracy through military coups, personal dictatorships, and monist party control, rather than leading to reform. Even revolutions often ended in single-party control. The dominant spirit of the times was not to foster "deliberation" and forge consent, nor to allow space for dissent, but to repress. As Cammack *et al.* (1993: 129) have written, "It is the closeness of party and state which accounts most satisfactorily for the failure of competitive liberal democracy to develop out of existing party systems in the Third World. It also accounts for the fact that change tends to come (if at all) in violent or at least in unconstitutional ways." Reform movements were all too often sacrificed on the "altar of stability." During the Cold War, the stability factor offered many third-world elite and military juntas an excuse for consolidating their power undemocratically, finding also ready approval among the Western powers who were concerned largely with preventing pro-Soviet governments from gaining power. Competitive democracy, which is messy, was often abandoned for stability.

The end of ideology, political pragmatism, and the adoption recently of more competitive political structures by many of the new democracies bode well for economic development also. The findings here do not support those who suggest that the adoption of democratic institutions is likely to lead to economic failure, and thereby pave the way for the reversal of recent democratic gains. Social scientists and the policy community, however, need to understand more clearly the costs and benefits of differing institutional reforms without pushing vague notions of "democracy," "empowerment," "decentralization," and "participation" as processes likely to cure economic woes. "All good things go together," but we must first distinguish carefully what exactly the good are from the bad. Achieving "good democracy" requires the application of liberty and discipline to both the governors and the governed. As James Madison argued in the *Federalist Papers 51*:

> If men were angels, no government would be necessary. If angels were to govern men, neither external nor internal government would be necessary. In framing a government which is to be administered by men over men, the great difficulty lies in this: you must first enable the government to control the governed; and in the next place oblige it to control itself.
>
> (Wills, 1982)

Stephen Holmes (1995: 135), in his spirited defense of liberal democracy, put it succinctly: "a constitution is Peter Sober, the electorate Peter Drunk." In many LDC democracies, the extent of democracy is encapsulated in men seeming like angels at election time to an electorate supplied with enough free booze. Without pushing catchwords such as "empowerment" and "participation," the donor community has a role to play in carefully evaluating the types of constitutional arrangements and institutional structures that strike the right balance between allowing governance and constraining rent seeking from the collusive elite and the convulsive mass. Institutions could certainly be crafted to nudge democracy in directions that allow consensual policymaking, sincere debate, protection of minority opinion, and the access to institutions and processes that foster democratic citizenship. The question for global policy is no longer whether or not democracy should be supported and nurtured but what about democratic institutions should be emphasized to achieve good public policy outcomes. Democracy does not just have to be "intrinsically" valuable. The universal appeal of democracy does not just come from aesthetics, but history shows it also works well for people's economic well-being.

Globalization and democracy

In this section, the question of FDI, trade, and democracy is addressed with Granger causality tests and pooled cross-sectional time-series models. I use the ratio of FDI stock to GDP, rather than flows, which are the most often used in similar studies. I continue to measure openness to trade as the influence of imports and exports within the economy (imports + exports/GDP) rather than trade policy. The question is, does being dependent on trade, or in the language of dependency or world-system theory, being subject to the vagaries of the capitalist world system, hinder democratization? I focus on the reality of trade dependence and not the potential in terms of trade policy, since I am interested in the structural effects crucial to globalization arguments. The data on trade-to-GDP ratios are taken from the Global Development Network (GDN) economic growth data set and are logged to correct skewness (Easterly and Sewadeh, 2001). The influence of foreign cpaital within an economy can be gauged by new investments (flows) or the accumulated influence of stock. I use accumulated stock, again for theoretical reasons concerning long-term effects of MNC "penetration" since stock tration" since stock ca ptures the "foothold" of MNCs to a greater degree than do flows alone. I am interested in the "lasting relationship" between FDI and a host society. The larger the ratio of stock to GDP, the greater the imprint of international actors (for good or evil) within an economy. Both measures proxy aspects of internationalization, or globalization, of an economy and capture different dimensions of the debate on economic freedom and democracy as discussed above.

The data on FDI stocks are already described in Chapter 3. Instead of stock estimates in 1970, 1980, and 1990, we now have stock data for each year since 1970 until 1999. I estimate stocks from 1970 to 1980 by subtracting flows reported by the World Bank (World Bank, 2001), which are derived from IMF balance of payments statistics. I estimate stock to 1999 by adding flows, using the 7 percent per annum rate of depreciation. My stock estimates for 1990 and 1999 (two points in time for which the UN reports stock) are highly correlated with figures reported by the UN ($r = 0.98$ [N = 104]). Thus, my method of estimating stock yields figures extremely close to the UN's. The GDP data are also taken from the GDN data set. I continue to use the Vanhanen index of democracy as my preferred measure of democracy.

I employ a pooled cross-section, time-series dataset for roughly 100 countries, measured annually between the years 1970 to 1999 to test the causal relationship between democracy, trade, and FDI. The data are unbalanced, meaning that there are missing data for some countries for some years. This is not a hindrance to model estimation. I first employ Granger causality tests to establish direction of causality between democracy and my globalization variables—trade and FDI—and then utilize a fuller model of democratization including relevant controls utilizing a pooled cross-section, time-series method to test the robustness of the relationship. The major question is, what are the grounds for optimistic and pessimistic scenarios on economic liberalization and the future of democracy?

Initially, I conduct Granger causality analyses to establish the direction of the causal arrow. The test demonstrates whether or not past values of one variable have a statistically significant impact on present-day values of a second variable, controlling for past values of the second variable (Granger, 1969, 1988). If the past values of the first variable exhibit a statistically significant effect, then the first variable is said to have "Granger-caused" the second variable. I test four possible causal directions:

1 trade Granger-causes democracy
2 democracy Granger-causes trade
3 FDI Granger-causes democracy
4 democracy Granger-causes FDI

To take the first causal direction, trade Granger-causes democracy, if democracy is affected by past values of trade, controlling for past values of democracy. If trade's effect is statistically significant, then trade is said to have "Granger-caused" democracy. Mathematically, the unrestricted model, denoted as:

$$\text{Democ}_t = a + b_1 \text{Trade}_{t-1} + b_2 \text{Democ}_{t-1} + b_3 \text{Democ}_{t-2} + b_i \text{Democ}_{ti} + \mu$$

where b_i = parameters to be estimated; μ = error term, should reveal a statistically significant F-test for the addition of the Trade_{t-1} variable, as opposed to the restricted model, denoted as:

$$\text{Democ}_t = a + b_1 \text{Democ}_{t-1} + b_2 \text{Democ}_{t-2} + b_i \text{Democ}_{ti} + \mu$$

where terms are defined as above. If trade flows are "Granger-caused" by democracy, then the unrestricted model, denoted as:

$$\text{Trade}_t = a + b_1 \text{Democ}_{t-1} + b_2 \text{Trade}_{t-1} + b_3 \text{Trade}_{t-2} + b_i \text{Trade}_{ti} + \mu$$

where b_∞ = parameters to be estimated; μ = error term, should reveal a statistically significant F-test for the addition of the $\text{Democ}_{t v1}$ variable, as opposed to the restricted model, denoted as:

$$\text{Trade}_t = a + b_1 \text{Trade}_{t-1} + b_2 \text{Trade}_{t-2} \ldots + b_i \text{Trade}_{ti} + \mu$$

where the terms are defined as above. This method is repeated for testing the direction of causality between democracy and FDI.

A critical issue to resolve when using Granger causality tests is the number of lags of the dependent and independent variables used to perform the test. If there are too few lags, the test will be inconsistent, but if there are too many lags, the test will be inefficient (Burkhart and Lewis-Beck, 1994). Several methods exist for determining the proper number of lags. The one that has been found to be the best performer by several researchers is the Final Prediction Error test, or FPE (Mahdavi and Sohrabian, 1991: 44–5). Using the FPE method, I determined that the following equations represent the optimal lag structure for the Granger causality tests.

$$Democ_t = a + b_1 \, Trade_{t-1} + b_2 \, Democ_{t-1} + \mu$$
$$Trade_t = a + b_1 \, Democ_{t-1} + b_2 \, Trade_{t-1} + \mu$$
$$Democ_t = a + b_1 \, FDI_{t-1} + b_2 \, Democ_{t-1} + \mu$$
$$FDI_t = a + b_1 \, Democ_{t-1} + b_2 \, FDI_{t-1} + b_3 \, FDI_{t-2} + \mu$$

An important point to remember about Granger tests is that they are bivariate, that is, no other variables can be held constant. For this reason, I test only the developing countries in my Granger tests, given the very large gap in wealth and levels of democracy between the rich and poor states. What I want to know is how trade and FDI affect the development of democracy within the poor countries as a group.

Table 5.3 reports the results from the Granger causality tests. As seen there, the causal effect of trade-to-GDP ratio on democracy is statistically significant at the 5 percent level, but trade's long-run effect on democracy is negative.[8] In other words, trade dependence does not statistically "predict" higher levels of democracy more than previous values of democracy

Table 5.3 Bivariate Granger causality results, democracy, trade, and FDI, 1970–98 (LDCs only)

Potential causal relationship tested	Long-run effect (in brackets) and F-test for Granger causal relationship
Trade to GDP ratio → Democracy	[−3.5] F = 16.77* (1,2284)
Democracy → Trade to GDP ratio	[0.03] F = 3.65 (1,2275)
FDI stock to GDP ratio → Democracy	[9.39] F = 48.14* (1,2207)
Democracy → FDI stock to GDP ratio	[−0.04] F = 3.92* (2,2119)

Notes
a Where * = statistical significance at 0.05 level, two-tailed test.
b Figures in parentheses are the degrees of freedom for the F-test. The long-run effect is calculated as the sum of coefficients of the independent variable divided by 1 minus the sum of coefficients of the lagged dependent variable.

predict itself. The reverse relationship, on the other hand, is statistically not different from zero—democracy does not Granger-cause higher trade-to-GDP ratios among the LDCs. This result, on the surface at least, seems to suggest that democracy does not increase trade as many suggest, but since I measure trade as dependence (total trade to GDP), the ratio is dependent on the denominator (GDP) as well, which I cannot control for in these tests. Therefore, I can only conclude that democracy does not discernibly Granger-cause higher trade dependence. Since these tests are only bivariate and lack important controls, like level of wealth and "gravity" factors, such as distance to major markets and size of domestic market, I cannot make strong claims about trade and democracy except to say that reciprocal causation statistically is weak and mixed. I address this issue in theoretically more pleasing terms by testing multivariate time-series, cross-section models below, which allows me to control other factors.

Moving on to the causal relationship between democracy and FDI, I find reciprocal causality between democracy and the level of MNC influence in economies. FDI stock-to-GDP Granger-causes democracy, and the long-run effect is positive, a result that is statistically significant at the 5 percent level. FDI shows a small long-run impact on democracy, which is positive. A percentage-point increase in the FDI stock to GDP ratio increases democracy on the Vanhanen index by 0.1, or 1/10 of a point. This is not entirely insignificant, given that the mean value for democracy among the LDCs is only 12.5 in the time-series data. A standard deviation increase would raise the democracy score by 1.2 points. The reverse relationship, democracy to the ratio of FDI stock to GDP, is also statistically significant, with the long-run effect showing a negative association. Increasing democracy by 1 point decreases the influence of MNCs in an economy by 4 percent. Since FDI to GDP ratio is dependent on the denominator, as it was with trade, we can only conclude from this result that democracy decreases dependence on FDI, a finding that should not be too surprising as FDI itself indirectly allows countries to become less dependent on it by boosting the rate of increase of the denominator, GDP. Moreover, democracy's association with growth and its influence on increasing domestic investment should also reduce dependence on foreign capital. The major point of these results for my interests is that the dependence of poor countries on FDI is not detrimental to democracy among the poor countries.

My results certainly do not show that MNCs influence oligarchic structures associated with autocracy as dependency and world-system theorists predicted, nor support the pessimistic arguments in the current debate on globalization and democracy. Contrarily, these tests lend preliminary support to propositions that view FDI as a "progressive" influence as some claim (Kobrin, 1976; Becker *et al.*, 1987). From a Granger causality perspective, trade seems problematic. However, the robustness of any relationship between FDI, trade, and democracy is dependent on what factors are controlled for, given FDI and trade's association with income and other "good things" that are associated with democracy.

Having established directions of causality, I test the robustness of the association between my main independent variables and democracy by including other structural variables in a pooled cross-section, time-series framework. Since the connection between FDI, trade, and democracy is usually presented as an indirect one through economic development, industrialization, and urbanization (modernization), I control for these variables in addition to historical and cultural/institutional factors. I control for social fractionalization, colonial history, and oil dependence following important recent theoretical and empirical work on democratization (Karl, 1997; Ross, 2001). FDI and trade dependence are also theoretically linked to historical factors such as colonial heritage and system of law. I do not expect to see much FDI or trade dependence in socialist systems, for example. Therefore, I control for legal systems, which are broken down into British, French, German, Socialist, and Scandinavian legal traditions, and these variables also roughly proxy for colonial heritage thought to be important for democracy.[9] These categorizations are obtained from the GDN growth data set. I control for ethnolinguistic fractionalization, which is often discussed as being problematic for democracy (Lijphart, 1977; Diamond and Plattner, 1994).[10]

Recent theoretical work on democracy highlights the problem of resource wealth (Karl, 1997). Political elites that have the luxury of "unearned income" allow state institutions around taxation to wither, which invariably leads to weak states that are unable to cope with economic and social crises. When resources yield high rents, state leaders do not have the incentives to provide public goods that enhance the chances of democracy, but may use the state as personal patrimony. Resource rents may also help to create factional political states with a high degree of societal conflict, so that democracy is emasculated.[11] Ross (2001) investigated whether the problematic relationship between Islam and democracy was really the effect of oil wealth and democracy and finds independent effects of oil and Islam on lower levels of democracy.[12] Others too report a significant negative effect of Islam on democracy, even if Islamic societies tend to have less inequality (Barro, 2001). FDI and trade-to-GDP ratios are intimately related to oil wealth, so I control for both oil wealth and religion in my models. Naturally, I capture many favorable aspects of democratization by including the logged value of per capita income, which should capture all the modernization and industrialization aspects beyond my liberal variables. The basic model is:

$$\text{Democ} = \beta_0 + \beta_1(\text{income}_{it}) + \beta_2(\text{FDI}_{it}) + \beta_3(\text{trade}_{it}) + \beta_4(\text{vector of legal systems}_{it}) + \beta_5(\text{vector of religions}_{it}) + \beta_6(\text{ethnolinguistic fraction}_{it}) + \beta_7(\text{oil export-dependence}) + \beta_8(\% \text{ urban pop.}) + \beta_{it} + e_{it}$$

I performed model estimation using the AR1(TSCS) procedure in the statistical package TSP 4.4. This maximum likelihood estimation procedure controls for autocorrelation through differencing each observation by the transformation Vt – rho (Vt –1) where V is the observation and rho is the autocorrelation coefficient (or the regression coefficient of the lagged error term). Parameter estimates are consistent, efficient, and readily interpretable as they are in the original metric of the variables in the model.

In Table 5.4, I present the results for the cross-section time-series analyses where I control for level of income, degree of urbanization, and historic and social factors. I present results for equations with FDI and trade individually and together. Column 1 shows that FDI has a positive and statistically significant impact on democracy, despite several statistically significant control variables that are strong. A percentage increase in the ratio of FDI to GDP predicts an increase in democracy of 0.044, but a standard deviation increase could boost the democracy score by 0.53, *ceteris paribus*.[13] What is interesting is, holding many other factors constant, dependence on FDI has a small positive "direct" effect on democracy.

The results of the control variables are also interesting. Per capita income is positively and statistically significantly related to democracy, results that support a host of other studies discussed above. Urbanization has a strong impact on democracy in the expected direction.[14] A standard deviation increase in the percentage of population that is urban can increase democracy by 5.5 points. This is generally strong support for modernization theory. A surprising finding is that the larger the share in the population of people classified as being Protestant, the smaller the score on democracy.

Two points are significant here. The first is that the democracy score favors fractionalized party systems (the Vanhanen value on competition is biased against two-party systems), which means that holding other factors constant, countries with a large share of any religious grouping could have a negative relationship with democracy, given that religious affiliation captures the degree to which society is plural. The second possibility is that since legal systems are held constant (all of them being from largely Protestant countries), the net effect of Protestantism per se is negative, compared to the institutional factors captured by the legal variables.[15] Both factors could also be at play. However, just dropping the dummy variable for Scandinavian legal system changes the sign on the share of the Protestant population, but its effect is insignificant. Although these relationships need further examination, I conclude here that culture seems to matter less than do institutions. Larger Catholic populations and larger Islamic populations are also negatively, and statistically, significantly related to democracy.

Interestingly, holding the other variables at their mean values, a standard deviation increase in each of the religions shows that Islam could reduce democracy by roughly twice the amount compared to the two other religious variables. Clearly, further study of this relationship is needed

Table 5.4 FDI, trade, and democracy, 1970–98 (all countries)

Variables	(1)	(2)	(3)	(4)
FDI stock/GDP	4.4*		5.2†	4.9†
	(1.9)		(2.1)	(2.0)
Trade/GDP (log)		−0.008	−0.45	−0.48
		(−0.008)	(−0.42)	(−0.44)
Income/pc (log)	2.4†	1.7*	2.4†	2.4†
	(2.5)	(1.9)	(2.5)	(2.3)
% Urban population	0.23§	0.26§	0.23§	0.23§
	(6.7)	(7.8)	(6.6)	(6.4)
% Protestant population	−0.12†	−0.12†	−0.12†	−0.12†
	(2.2)	(−2.1)	(−2.2)	(−2.3)
% Catholic population	−0.053*	−0.055*	−0.050*	−0.047
	(−1.8)	(−1.9)	(−1.8)	(−1.6)
% Muslim population	−0.13§	−0.13§	−0.13§	−0.12§
	(−4.3)	(−4.5)	(−4.3)	(−4.1)
Ethnolinguistic fractionalization	−3.1	−3.1	−3.1	−2.9
	(−1.2)	(−1.3)	(−1.2)	(−1.2)
British legal system	1.09	1.4	1.2	1.5
	(0.64)	(0.81)	(0.71)	(0.58)
Socialist legal system	−6.1	−6.0	−6.1	−3.8
	(−1.6)	(−1.6)	(−1.6)	(−0.98)
German legal system	9.5†	9.8†	9.5†	9.7†
	(2.5)	(2.6)	(2.5)	(2.6)
Scandinavian legal system	18.8§	18.4§	19.1§	19.7§
	(3.5)	(−3.4)	(3.6)	(3.6)
Oil dependent	−7.5§	−7.0§	−7.5§	−7.5§
Oil > 50% exports	(−3.1)	(−3.0)	(−3.2)	(−3.2)
Growth of GDP				0.0052
				(0.54)
Cold War period dummy				−0.55*
				(−1.7)
Constant	−0.37	1.3	0.18	0.56
	(−0.09)	(0.30)	(0.04)	(0.13)
Adjusted R²	0.94	0.94	0.94	0.93
D-W	1.7	1.7	1.7	1.7
Rho	0.93	0.93	0.93	0.93
N	2748	2759	2688	2597
States	99	100	99	97
Log likelihood	−7063.7	−7098.5	−6936.3	−6726

Notes

t-ratios in parentheses
§ denotes statistical significance at the 0.001 level
† denotes statistical significance at the 0.05 level
* denotes statistical significance at the 0.10 (two-tailed tests)
N denotes number of cases in analysis
States denotes number of states in analysis.

through the testing of alternative measures of democracy. In any case, if these results are an artifact of the way in which Vanhanen's index is derived, it is further confirmation as to why democracy might be easier to accomplish in fractionalized, rather than moderately homogenous societies and why indeed democracy should encourage pluralistic structures. There is possibly some linkage between religious homogeneity and the inability to democratize with the fact that moderately fractionalized societies also experience more civil conflict (Collier and Hoeffler, 2000; de Soysa, 2002). The anti-democratic Islamic effect, of course, is confirmed in other carefully constructed studies focused on this particular topic (Ross, 2001).[16] Further study is clearly needed to evaluate what type of democratic institutions are best suited for increasing democracy while lowering the incidence of conflict.

Surprisingly, the term for ethnolinguistic fractionalization is not significantly different from zero. Ethnicity does not seem to matter in terms of the level of democracy, perhaps reflecting again the nature of Vanhanen's index, which captures social pluralism in the competition component. This result too points at why there might be more normative value of democracy conceptualized and measured in terms of polyarchy given that greater competition might be reflecting greater representativeness in an ethnically plural system. Interestingly, the British legal system is insignificantly related to democracy, while the German and Scandinavian systems are positive and highly significant. This result might also be reflecting the fact that British systems generally favor two-party, Westminster-style democracy. Moreover, since Britain and France had the largest share of colonies, the history of postcolonial societies is reflected in this result. The socialistic legal system is negatively related to democracy and approaches statistical significance at the 10 percent level. As reported by others, being oil dependent is extremely unfavorable for democracy. Being dependent on oil reduces the level of democracy by 7.5 points, just short of the mean value for all LDC democracies. It seems that Islam and oil wealth are an unfortunate mix when it comes to democratization, but then so might it be for oil and Catholicism as exemplified by the unhappy history of Venezuela and Mexico in Latin America, or Angola and Zaire in Africa.

Column 2 leaves out FDI and tests trade on democracy independently. Trade's effect on democracy is very slightly negative but fails statistical significance.[17] The control variables are little changed. In column 3, adding both FDI and trade in the model, FDI is still positive and significant statistically. Including a dummy variable for the Cold War era (dummy coded as 1 if year falls between 1970 and 1989 and 0 if after 1989) and the growth of GDP exhibits little effect on my primary variables of interest (col. 4). As expected, the Cold War era was unfavorable for democracy, but growth's effect is statistically insignificant. I tested several variants of these models, adding several other variables such as size of the population, but the basic results on FDI and trade remained unchanged. FDI to GDP remained robust to specification. Trade was always statistically insignificant, but at no time was it close to being negative and significant as expected by pessimists. It seems that the Granger causality effects of trade dependence on democracy do not hold when controls are included. Further research should decompose trade dependence to tease out possible differential effects from manufacturing and primary commodity dependence on democracy, given the strong association between primary commodity dependence and other adverse outcomes, such as lower economic growth and the onset of civil war (Collier and Hoeffler, 2000; Sachs and Warner, 2001).

6 Assessing globalization's correlates and concomitants

Summary, conclusions, and implications

There is little doubt that the concept of globalization—the word on everyone's lips—will dominate global politics well into the 21st century. Judging by the recent discussions at the Earth Summit 2002 held in Johannesburg, South Africa, concerns over globalization and questions of economic and political development in particular will surely heighten in the coming decades. The end of the Cold War that dominated world politics for the latter half of the previous century, which saw superpower competition and ideological schism that artificially divided societies and devoured unimaginable resources, was only momentarily heralded as the "end of history." People expected a peace dividend, but the reality, brought home today by a globalized media, is still one of great deprivation and suffering for too many around the world. Today, 10 years after the world embarked on saving the environment, it has become apparent that poverty itself is a major culprit of environmental degradation (Lomborg, 2001). However, globalization as an answer has been seriously challenged, and activists are galvanized against it on the ground floor of life, while the philosophers and academic theorists are engaged in battles of words on the "upper floors." Some have even interpreted the events of September 11 as the first shots fired in a "clash of globalizations" where it is blamed for new "conflicts and resentments" resulting from social injustice and exclusion, rather than the often touted promise of integration (Hoffmann, 2002: 111).

This study has sought to bring some perspective to what is meant by globalization, measuring its contours and assessing its correlates and concomitants. I have tried to show that the debate on globalization, largely at the level of polemics, has theoretical precedents in the form of older debates between modernization and dependency or world-systems theories, discussions that dominated the field of development. Such discussions have been particularly lively among political scientists, sociologists, and scholars of development studies, whose theoretical and empirical concerns rarely bothered mainstream economists as much as the debate on globalization has more recently, despite the similarities in concerns. While the ideological gloss has largely faded from the rhetoric, the bases of the arguments are the same. For the globalization pessimists, increasing trade and the spread of MNCs are exploitative—economically and socially—because they undermine the chances of poor countries to raise income and develop democracy. Proponents of globalization see FDI as a vehicle for economic growth, and the spread of market capitalism as the surest way to consolidated democracy. This book has occupied itself mainly with these concerns, addressing the theory and utilizing the latest available hard data covering a large number of countries for testing the propositions. I summarize my results below.

This study has chosen to define globalization minimally, given that it has come to mean everything and nothing. What is truly significant about this era of globalization is the simultaneous spread of democracy and market capitalism, a widely accepted definition (Munck and Gills, 2002). Here I have conceptualized globalization on the bases of its economic foundations—FDI and trade—and the political and social bases, which are the near universal adoption of democracy among territorial states. All too often, scholars tend to juxtapose the economic (capitalism) against the political (communitarianism-socialism), equating the loud protest on the street with everything that is good, particularly for the poor world, and the spread of FDI to developing countries as imperialistic, reflected in the interests and greed of the multilateral lending agencies and the rich countries. Such claims are not just from the "man on the street" but come with heavy scholarly credentials. James Mittelman spoke for many when he wrote, "There is a clash emerging between two models: neo-liberal globalization, which at present is the dominant force, and democratic globalization, a far less coherent counterforce" (Mittelman, 1997: 241). Moreover, concerns over the ultimate fate of unrestrained neoliberal globalization are encapsulated in statements such as the following: "[globalization] is intensified colonialism, even though it is under an unfamiliar guise" (Miyoshi, 1993: 750).

I addressed the issue of foreign capital and economic growth, democracy and economic growth, and the compatibility of foreign capital and democracy by utilizing the latest investment data and a sounder operationalization than previous studies. The results obtained here, based on evidence garnered over the three decades covering 1970–99, do not provide any cause for pessimism about FDI and growth and the more controversial relationship between democracy and growth. Moreover, I find enough evidence to disprove pessimistic views on the future of democracy given the spread of foreign capital and trade. I have closely followed the methodology of previous studies that gauged the effects of foreign capital and democracy on economic growth, demonstrating that the new data and the application of theoretically satisfying testing procedures yield highly promising results. The problem with previous studies has been that democracy was neither conceptualized properly in relation to why it matters for growth, nor tested empirically with measures that capture the precise dimension of democracy linked to growth.

After testing several major propositions and related hypotheses, I find that FDI and trade promote growth. A sounder operationalization of democracy yields positive effects on growth that are statistically significant, independently of the usual controls, results that refute some major studies upon which the empirical consensus that democracy is unimportant for economic development rests (Barro, 1998; Przeworski *et al.*, 2000). However, the results show support for a synthesized view of pessimistic and optimistic expectations, but much depends on how democracy is conceptualized and measured. My results support a conceptualization of democracy that also carries normative concerns about what qualities of democracies have value, both intrinsic and extrinsic. I find that what is in fact normatively valuable about democracy, as discussed by those interested in qualitative aspects of democracy, also affects extrinsic values such as promoting faster rates of growth. This is good news for designers of democracy.

In the case of foreign capital and economic growth, this study finds evidence to refute the notion that states that are more dependent on foreign capital will grow more slowly. The "penetration" by MNCs of an economy is not detrimental to poor countries. In fact, foreign and domestic capital flows have spurred growth to a degree similar to that reported by studies covering other periods of time using different data (Dixon and Boswell, 1996b; Firebaugh, 1996; de Soysa and Oneal, 1999). This result is interesting and reflects the constancy of the degree to which investment takes place among countries viewed cross-nationally. In other words, given no adventitious circumstances, most states probably receive investment at comparatively constant rates, perhaps foreign investment to lesser degrees than domestic. The new data show a more plausible position, which is that higher ratios of domestic capital to GDP are positively and significantly related to growth, but since domestic capital accumulates faster than foreign capital and is the major source of capital within poor countries, this result is hardly surprising. Moreover, since FDI encourages domestic capital investment and does not displace it, FDI possibly increases growth indirectly by encouraging the faster accumulation of domestic capital as well (de Soysa and Oneal, 1999).

The differential effect of foreign and domestic capital as reflected in the size of the coefficient has previously been interpreted by some to mean that foreign capital is bad for economic growth as dependency theorists predicted (Dixon and Boswell, 1996a). The less pessimistic evaluation of this finding is that it has been "less good" than domestic capital (Firebaugh, 1992). These conclusions, however, are not entirely accurate, if "less good" is interpreted more meaningfully. Domestic capital is better at creating growth only because there is much more of it. Given the disparities of the amounts of flow and accumulated stock of the two forms of capital

(29 to 1 in the data analyzed here), foreign capital is roughly 2.5 times better for growth, dollar for dollar, a reinterpretation offered by de Soysa and Oneal (1999) and confirmed by these results covering a 30-year period. The problem, in fact, seems to be that foreign capital is much less globalized than most people are wont to believe. It picks the favorable areas within which to locate.

The problem clearly is that foreign capital is not running rampant in the developing world, as I demonstrated earlier in this book. The spread of FDI is taking place extremely unevenly, and it seems to avoid those areas that are being marginalized, precisely for conditions that keep these areas underdeveloped because of the inability to attract both FDI and domestic capital. Such factors as low human and institutional development, bad governance, and conflict all contribute to create the vicious cycle of low levels of investment and net outflows of capital from much of the poor world, particularly from sub-Saharan Africa (Collier and Gunning, 1999). Foreign capital is highly discerning and chooses its location based on favorable environments. It seems that the preferred location for the bulk of foreign capital that flows around the globe is within the already rich areas and among a small group of rapidly developing countries. What has taken place steadily since the 1960s and 1970s when the LDCs were highly hostile to liberal, open-market economics and FDI, when LDCs resorted to massive expropriation in the guise of nationalism and ISI strategies, coupled with technological and sociopolitical factors, has been what some, such as Hoogvelt (2001), refer to as the "reconcentration" of capital, or capital deepening, among the richer states. The recent trends, however, are promising, since the developing areas have begun gradually to increase their share of FDI, largely due to a pragmatic approach to foreign invest-ment exemplified most starkly by countries such as China, Vietnam, and even Cuba.

One might ask, is this a good thing for consolidating freedom? This study also addressed the second pillar of this wave of globalization. Does the spread of democracy complement market liberalization for generating economic growth? I approached the subject differently compared to the scores of others who have used regime type dichotomously as democracies and autocracies. I argued that the answer to the "empirical puzzle" as to the conflicting evidence of democracy and growth lies in differentiating good democracies from badly functioning ones, or testing qualitative aspects of democracy on growth. I related the two visions of democracy—majoritarian and proportional—to the question of growth, connecting these qualitative aspects of the various theories as to why regime type matters for growth. My results support a synthesized view of the optimist and pessimist camps. The answer to the question of whether democracy promotes growth seems to depend on the question "What is meant by democracy?" This question is as old as the science of politics (Dahl, 2000).

I conceptualized democracy as polyarchy, which allows one to gauge

degrees of "democracy" among countries on dimensions that have normative value and to connect "democracy" in practice theoretically to why it
matters for growth. By culling the large and disparate bodies of theory on
regimes and growth, I specified that the competitive aspects of democracy
should promote growth over features that may be democratic, by standard
measure, but not necessarily competitive. My hypothesis that it is competitive aspects of democracy (the degree of contestation) that matter for
economic growth is supported when testing the issue empirically with
objective data, which measure the two dimensions of democracy that make
a polyarchy. The inclusiveness of participation measured in terms of electoral data, holding constant the degree to which the political process is
contestable, has negative effects on growth, particularly among the poorer
countries. The results are instructive for constitutional designers and
policymakers. If democracy is to have extrinsic value, the answer is not to
simply promote electoral democracy but to insure democratic design that
promotes greater avenues for contestation. Institutional guarantees for life,
liberty, and property are inherently politically derived, and institutional
arrangements that promote consensual decisionmaking, meaningful choice,
and participation, and allow oversight of political leadership beyond retrospective voting, seem also to be valuable for generating growth. It seems
that the current consensus, which views democracy as unimportant for
growth, rests on shaky empirical grounds.

The implications of these findings are quite profound. On the one hand,
they confirm the optimistic view, which is that democracy is compatible
with economic growth. On the other hand, they support the pessimistic
views on mass participation as well. The fundamental message, however, is
that "good" and "bad" democracies, in terms of economic growth, are
identifiable on theoretical and measurable grounds and the results speak to
larger discussions about the two visions of democracy. These results also
illuminate the question as to why most of the LDCs at one time adopted
socialist policies of redistribution and instituted statist policies rather than
integrate with the global market (Sachs and Warner, 1995a, 1995b). In
fact, a cursory glance back shows that the development failures have been
those societies that decolonized through mass movements that had mobilized against colonial rule, whether it be India under Mahatma Gandhi and
Jawaharlal Nehru, or Egypt under Gamal Abdel Nasser. The same might
be said for the many popular African leaders, such as Kwame Nkrumah of
Ghana, whose recipe for development was "seek ye first the political
kingdom." The economic successes, however, were those societies, such as
in Japan, Korea, Taiwan, and Singapore that were highly restrained for a
variety of reasons, where the state elites found high degrees of insulation
from popular demands and were able to build cross-class coalitions that
were stable.

The recent instabilities resulting from the dissolution of the Soviet
"empire" serve as a clear example of the incapacity of state institutions to

handle transitions of such magnitude, while trying to build a new society, state institutions, and economic well-being at the same time. As is suggested by some political scientists, however, democracies can be "crafted" to be more competitive, with the adoption, for example, of proportional representation electoral systems, the promotion of multipartyism, separation of powers, federalism, etc. There may be many more instruments beyond constitutions and electoral systems to design ways in which policymaking power becomes diffuse and where citizen input into policymaking can be made both effective and representative. While I have not identified exact links from party systems, fractionalization, or polarization and other such relevant topics in relation to growth, the development of new data sets on political institutions will facilitate future research on this crucial topic (Beck *et al.*, 2001).

An important concomitant of globalization is the growth of democracy. I addressed this issue by visiting some earlier theoretical issues concerning the influence of international capitalist forces on the level of democracy. My crucial globalization variables are the stock of FDI (accumulated capital) to GDP and imports plus exports (total trade) to GDP. First, I tested for direct causality using Granger causality analysis and found FDI to have statistically significant causal effects on democracy to a greater degree than the other way around. I did not establish such an effect with trade openness. However, FDI seemed to be robustly related to democracy in pooled cross-sectional time-series models controlling for other salient factors effecting democracy. Trade, which is correlated with FDI, is positively related to democracy but statistically significant only if FDI and urbanization are not in the model, which suggests that disaggregating trade may yield more realistic results. My results from the Granger causality tests and the cross-sectional time-series models taken together suggest that FDI and trade carry some direct and indirect benefits for poor countries.

These results call into question the heated debates on the structural effects of globalization on the democratic developmental prospects of poor countries. The way in which I operationalize my key variables, however, does not allow me to say conclusively that MNCs never try to subvert democratic processes to safeguard profits. After all, it may take just one or two companies to influence politics in a poor country for good or ill. What I can say is that the structural arguments do not hold up empirically. In fact, accumulated stock to GDP probably indicates certain positive aspects of the domestic environment that encourages FDI and thereby a competitive market environment, which also encourages democracy. Moreover, higher competition among the MNCs themselves should lead to less corrupt outcomes as they would seek to minimize collusion out of self-interest, calling for tighter controls and regulation of corrupt practices. The problem, as has often been the case, is the collusive tendencies between a government (ruling elite) and an MNC for extracting monopoly profits for themselves, which means that there should still be vigilance at the global level to hold MNCs and governments accountable, as the "global compact" and George Soros's recent initiative against MNC corruption seek to do.

While I can disprove the pessimistic expectations, further analysis is required to tease out the exact links from FDI to democracy. My suspicions are that free markets and local global linkages create the pressure on governments and companies to live up to the expectations of global consumers. If this is truly the case, then globalization has perhaps not gone far enough yet, and as one book title suggests, the antiglobalization, communitarian coalitions that see MNCs as all evil may in fact be "fighting the wrong enemy" (Graham, 2000). Moreover, while my measure of trade openness (the ratio of actual trade to GDP) is not directly a measure of liberal policy, but rather the extent of liberalization, perhaps trade and democracy's reciprocal relationships are overtheorized relative to FDI's relationship with democracy, a serious lacuna in the literature thus far. Clearly, future research should pay close attention to trade and FDI's reciprocal role with regard to democracy. These results, however, suggest that those who see contradictions in globalization may in fact be overstating it.

As some have argued, the sins of FDI may not be ones of "commission" but of "omission" (Gilpin, 1987: 301–3). The recent bill drafted by the US Congress, providing incentives to companies for investing in Africa is seemingly a reflection of doing something about this omission. The Europeans and others have also initiated several schemes, both bilaterally and through the WTO and GATT. The willingness of many countries to spurn FDI has also changed, and many are now competing to attract it, liberalizing their trade regimes and improving macro conditions, which I have demonstrated to have spillovers in positive ways in terms of enhancing the prospects also for democracy. Yet, such communitarian coalitions as those that galvanized against the MAI, which still claim greater protection for the poor world, seem to have won the day—there's been much backsliding and policymakers now seem to suggest that globalization should be "made to work" and that globalization should be democratized to serve people (DFID, 2000; Gills, 2002; Sklair, 2002). My results support others, who argue that it already does work, particularly within poor countries (Baghwati, 2000). Worryingly, it may be true that the disparate coalitions of protesters are beginning to influence political discourse in a direction that questions its efficacy for promoting development. The danger, I believe, is that Seattle and the noisy protests since have led to the "privatization" of policymaking, rather than to policymaking that steadily pushes liberalization of markets and promotes free trade (Baghwati, 2000).

While much of the debate on globalization centers on the effects of it on unskilled labor in the rich countries, I believe that the globally consequential problems stem from the problems of want facing the mass of humanity in poor societies. These wants are not just commodities, but institutions, policies, and good governance in general, factors that simultaneously keep many of these areas from becoming globalized. Finding the right policies to break the vicious cycles are the policy challenges facing global and local policymakers. The differences of opinion on whether or not globalization supports or hinders the development prospects of states have been based on the theoretical frameworks offered by liberal (modernization) theories and neo-Marxist (world-system) theories. I believe that the weight of the evidence, as I have tried to present above, supports the view that trade and foreign investment are likelier than not to benefit poor societies.

While the process of development never comes easily, economic growth does not necessarily have to be accompanied by great woe as even some modernization theorists believed during the disruptive days of the Cold War (Huntington, 1968). Many countries have made the transition from poor to middle income, or from poor to rich without too much disruption. The degree of disruption may depend heavily on the shape of political institutions that allow stable and consensual policymaking (Haggard, 1997; Rodrik, 1999). This observation also applies to the global polity, whose main task will be to balance out the interests of winners and losers in the globalization process in a consensual, deliberative, and considered manner. Democracy, after all, is symbiotic with the market because it allows antagonists to settle issues peacefully, where the strong and well placed do not always prevail because of organizational advantages that allow them to make the most noise.

"Democracy" and "imperialism" have been the most salient political terms of the 20th century with imperialism having gradually given way to democracy by the beginning of the 21st—we are in an era of "post-imperialism" (Becker *et al.*, 1987). It is certainly heartening that with more and more states and political leaders recognizing the promises of globalization that the right policy environments will be instituted to capture the benefits for ordinary people around the world. This factor, after all, is what eroded the postwar structure of bipolarity with all its attendant costs and has offered the world an array of options. The world is not united yet in one borderless marketplace, but it is an option that should be promoted for making the world more liveable. The rich countries have several policy options at their fingertips—if they want to avoid the spillovers of poverty, conflict, disease, and environmental destruction across the world. Retreat to nationalist policies, the subsidization of the already rich by providing farm subsidies, protecting the jobs of the rich by protecting markets, the imposition of import quotas on the poor, are the norms of the globalized world today, not unfettered markets. Improving the policy framework to change this situation is urgent, given that the problems facing the poor—from Mongolia to Managua—are no longer someone else's.

Data appendix

Variables and data

FDI stock 1970—obtained by subtracting flows from FDI inward stock reported for 1980 in UNCTAD, 2001. A 5 percent per annum depreciation rate was used, keeping with the method used by others (Ballmer-Cao and Scheidegger, 1979; Firebaugh, 1992). The 1980 stock figure was converted to constant 1996 dollars using the US GDP deflator (the seasonally adjusted yearly GDP deflator is available from the Federal Reserve Bank of St. Louis—http://research.stlouisfed.org/fred/data/gdp/gdpdef). The FDI flows were obtained from the World Bank's World Development Indicators (WDI) (2001), which were also converted to 1996$.

FDI stock 1990 and 1999—obtained by adding flows to stock 1980. The same depreciation rate as that noted above was used. The flows were also taken from the World Bank.

Domestic stock 1970, 1980, 1990 and 1999—obtained by accumulating flows of investment from 1960 to 1970 using Easterly and Sewadeh's (2001) investment-to-GDP ratio. I then computed the dollar value in 1996$ for each year's flows, using their total GDP estimates for each of those years. Domestic investment was computed as total investment minus FDI. I also used a 5 percent depreciation rate as with the FDI variables when adding flows to the estimated stock of 1970. The 10-year accumulating period is consistent with UNCTAD's estimating procedure for many countries where FDI stock in 1980 was unavailable.

All GDP per capita figures, size of total GDP, trade-to-GDP ratios, and the three components of human capital (secondary schooling, fertility, and under-five mortality) were obtained from Easterly and Sewadeh (2001), supplemented with data from the World Bank's WDI (2001). The fertility and under-five mortality rates are largely from UNICEF (2001). The following data points were not available in these three sources: The data on secondary education and fertility rate for Taiwan were estimated as the average of Hong Kong's and South Korea's (the United Nations does not report data on Taiwan).

Missing values for trade to GDP were taken from the Penn World Tables 5.6a[1] for the following:

- 1970 = Angola, Guinea, Ethiopia, Tanzania, Namibia, Mozambique, Seychelles, Zimbabwe, Panama, Bolivia, Iran, Yemen, Jordan, Cyprus, Germany, and Poland.
- 1980 = Tanzania, Qatar, Ethiopia, Angola, Guinea, Germany, and Yemen.
- 1990 = Germany and Sudan.

The GDP per capita growth rates for each of the three decades 1970–80, 1980–90, and 1990–9 were calculated by using the PPP based per capita income reported in Easterly and Sewadeh (2001) and fitting these values to a trend line following the least-squares method used by the World Bank (2002b). The equation is $x_t = a + b_t + e_t$ where x is the log of per capita income, a is the intercept, b is the parameter to be estimated, t is time, and e is the error term. The growth rate r is the [antilog (b)] −1. This method minimizes the influence of extreme values on the average growth rate.

Several important countries lack data in the Vanhanen index of democracy. The missing points for the following four countries, for each of the years 1970, 1980, and 1990 were unambiguously authoritarian as reflected in the Polity IV and the Freedom House index, therefore, I coded Hong Kong, Papua New Guinea, Namibia, and Zimbabwe as 0 for each panel year and in the time-series.

The dummy variable for the "core countries," which double up as industrialized democracies in Chapter 5 are USA, Great Britain, Canada, Australia, Austria, Belgium, Denmark, France, Finland, Germany, Greece, Iceland, Italy, Japan, Luxembourg, the Netherlands, Norway, New Zealand, Portugal, Spain, Sweden, and Switzerland.

The data for the time-series analyses are from Easterly and Sewadeh (2001) and the World Bank (2001). The legal systems and petroleum export dependence are dummy variables coded by Easterly and Sewadeh (2001).

The data on ethnolinguistic fractionalization and share of population of the major religions are from Kaufmann, Kraay, and Zoido-Lobaton (1999).

Table A.1 Summary statistics for cross-national growth empirics

Variable	N	Mean	St. dev.	Min.	Max.
Growth per capita	246	1.5	2.5	−8	9.6
FDI inv. rate	247	12.2	12.2	−13.3	76.5
FDI stock/GDP	247	10.9	14.6	0.05	86.3
Domestic inv. rate	247	7.1	3.3	−4	20.2
Domestic stock/GDP	247	202.6	116	51.7	960
Size (total GDP) log	247	10.2	1.9	6.4	15.3
Trade/GDP	247	68.6	48.9	9	379
Income per cap. log	247	7.9	1	5.8	9.9
Human capital	247	0.079	1.6	−3.3	2.7
Vanhanen democracy	247	12.9	13.3	0	44.2
Vanhanen competition	247	31.9	25.9	0	70
Vanhanen participation	247	29.2	21.2	0	68.3
Political rights (Gastil)	245	3.6	2.2	1	7
Polity IV	246	12.6	7.8	1	21
Economic freedom	210	5.7	1.6	1.9	9.7

Table A.2 Summary statistics for Granger causality and cross-national time-series analyses

Variable	N	Mean	St. dev.	Min.	Max.
Vanhanen democracy	2597	12.5	13.3	0	47.1
FDI stock/GDP	2597	0.10	0.012	0	1.1
Income per capita log	2597	3.3	0.6	2	4.9
Trade/GDP log	2597	1.7	0.025	0.57	2.7
Growth of GDP	2597	1.4	5.5	−39.5	34.3
% urban population	2597	48.1	24.4	2.4	100
% Protestant	2597	13.3	21.8	0	97.8
% Catholic	2597	38.7	37.7	0	96.9
% Islamic	2597	20.8	33.2	0	99.4
Ethnolinguistic fraction	2597	0.35	0.30	0	0.89

Notes

Introduction

1 There is much more to economic liberalization than FDI and trade. For example, capital market liberalization and the rapid expansion of portfolio investment are a complex subject, the effects of which are highly debated, see Baghwati (2000). I am interested in trade and FDI primarily because of their supposed structural effects on determining adverse outcomes within poor countries. Besides, most poor countries get little if any portfolio investment given the underdeveloped nature of capital markets and other risks.

2 Stiglitz (2002) engages in some hyperbole when he contends that globalization is being challenged everywhere, particularly in the LDCs. In fact, at no time since the end of colonialism have LDC governments and people been as favorable to foreign capital and open market principles as they are now. The gap in attitudes between most LDCs and the East and Southeast Asian pragmatists during the 1960s, 1970s, and 1980s was enormous. It is the latter group that Stiglitz lauds for being successful globalizers. He, like many policymakers, seems to have fallen prey to the loud discourse of grievance by treating it as broadly representative of the global citizenry.

3 See Schneider *et al.* (2003) for an evaluation of the theoretical and empirical evidence on the "liberal peace" idea and for a plea for extending empirical analyses as rigorously to other domains.

4 See also the debates in Munck and Gill (2002).

1 The contours of globalization

1 For an excellent overview of the debate, see Gilpin (2000), Held and McGrew (2000), and Nye and Donahue (2000). For an economic analysis of the effects of trade, focusing on the USA and North America, see Burtless *et al.* (1998). For a skeptical view on the benefits of globalization by an economist, see Rodrik (1997). On the question of globalization's effect on the state and on questions of democracy, see Armijo (1999) and Sakamoto (1994).

2 The best-known attack on globalization is Martin and Schumann (1997). Other critical accounts are Rodrik (1997), Gray (1999), Mittelman (2000).

3 See Bhagwati (1999) and Birdsall and Lawrence (1999) for discussions of the policy changes within poor countries regarding liberalization. Krasner (1985) provides an analysis of the evolution of the Group of 77 and the hostile stance of most poor countries to a liberal economic order during the 1960s and 1970s.

4 See, for example, Väyrynen (1999).

5 See Hoogvelt (2001) for a synthesis of various dependency and modernization positions.

6 Neo-Marxist, dependency arguments continue to be expounded by many, such as Amin (1990), Hettne (1995), Falk (1999), Mittelman (2000), Hoogvelt (2001).

7 Other sources, such as Russett and Oneal (2000) report a steady long-term decline after 1885, and with little or no evidence of globalization. Their aggregate figures are, however, based on whatever trade data are available for any given year and are probably also heavily influenced by the emergence of new states. Russett and Oneal themselves point out that information on trade (outside of the major powers) was underreported before the foundation of the IMF and OECD.

8 Low income countries and the OECD countries have the same average trade-to-GDP ratio. This of course does not mean that international trade cannot be important for well-being. This result simply means that rich countries contain larger domestic markets (GDP), which generally lowers the trade to GDP ratio.

9 Except where other sources are cited, the figures in this subsection are based on UNCTAD (2000), World Bank (2000), and my own calculations from these sources.

10 See Hoogvelt (2001) for similar statistics and conclusions.

11 Lane and Milesi-Ferretti's (2000) computation of external assets and liabilities finds the ratio of FDI stock to GDP between rich and poor countries to be roughly the same as mine.

12 I examine more closely the available measures of democracy in theoretical and empirical terms below.

13 In Figure 1.4, I use Vanhanen's measure of democracy, which puts more emphasis on participation than the others, and is therefore strongly influenced by suffrage, and shows a more dramatic increase over the long haul. However, the broad outline of the waves is very similar with the other measures as can be seen from Figure 1 in Vanhanen (2000).

14 Not all neoliberal economists agree with every facet of the argument presented here. However, there is very wide agreement that market forces and free trade—and the efficiency they promote—benefit LDCs; see Srinivasan and Baghwati (1999) for discussion on agreement and disagreements.

2 Globalization and development: theory old and new

1 It is estimated by the World Bank (1995) that the implementation of the GATT would increase the world's real income by $200 billion, a generous $179 billion of which is expected to benefit the LDCs.

2 Some scholars argue that the liberal democratic state as we know it is becoming superfluous under conditions of globalization. They suggest the importance of redefining processes of democracy to reflect these changes (Held 1995).

3 The term "structuralist" will be used to identify the neo-Marxist, dependency school of thought on development because of the general belief among the disparate dependency theorists that the structure of the world capitalist system leads to "underdevelopment" of poor countries (Frank 1969). The terms "dependency" and "structuralist" will be used interchangeably here.

4 It must be noted that not all neoliberal economists agree with each and every facet of the arguments that are presented here. However, there is a general consensus that market forces, free trade, and the efficiency they promote benefit LDCs.

5 Contrary to Lenin, who argued that the capital of imperialists flows to the periphery preceding military subjugation, the pattern of core capital flows of

the late 20th century resembles that of the late 19th. For an examination of British and US investments in their respective hegemonic periods, see Oneal (1988).

6 I discuss these highly complex theories merely to illustrate on what grounds the optimists and pessimists on foreign capital base their claims. These issues are taken up later in greater detail.

7 I discuss these theories and the empirical findings supporting them in greater detail below.

8 See Browett (1985) for an exposition of differing positions.

9 For a contemporary Marxist analysis of the "democratization" of capital and its progressive influence in the LDCs, see Warren (1980).

10 The various critiques, coming from all quarters, against assumptions and conclusions of the myriad dependency theories are not discussed here. For an excellent analysis of dependency theory and its critics, see Palma (1995).

11 It should be noted that Rodrik is generally favorable to FDI, suggesting that it may reduce corruption and strengthen the rule of law.

12 For detailed reviews of the plethora of theories on causes of democratization, see Huntington (1991) and Laitin (2000). Much work on democratization focused on transitions from authoritarianism, which focused on the strategic behavior of elites at the expense of structural factors (O'Donnell *et al.*, 1986). Some argue the need to renew attention to structural factors (Remmer, 1997). The debate on globalization and democracy is of course structurally based.

13 Frey *et al.* (1984) surveyed over 1,500 economists for their views on trade and found that 81 percent of the US economists agreed with the statement that "tariffs and quotas reduce general economic welfare." While 70 percent of German economists agreed, just 27 percent of French economists did (reported in Lewis-Beck, 1988). See Srinivasan and Baghwati (1999) for a discussion of disagreements over trade openness and economic growth. Policymakers are in a constant quandary balancing the needs of winners and losers in a situation that Bill Clinton referred to as a "three dimensional chess of trade" (Pfaff, 2001).

3 Globalization and growth empirics

1 Size is measured as total energy consumption in 1967 in thousand tons of coal equivalents because Bornschier and Chase-Dunn feel that this captures the size of the monetized part of the economy, leaving out the subsistence sector.

2 I use the accelerated depreciation method with a half-life of 10 years. I use World Bank flows because they are available in electronic form and are identical to those reported by the UN (r = 0.99).

4 Democracy and growth: theory old and new

1 See Aron (2000) and Dethier (1999) and useful surveys of the theoretical and empirical evidence on democracy, governance, and economic performance.

2 Nobel laureate Amartya Sen's view that democracy is intrinsically valuable even if it has no extrinsic value is testament to this consensus. It is also commonly argued that democracy has a positive indirect effect on growth through social stability and social investments that enhance human capital; see Tavares and Wacziarg (2001).

3 Rent seeking is the political manipulation of markets so that groups and individuals get more than what market forces will allocate. For example, farmers seek rents when they lobby government for higher tariffs on imported produce. Likewise, steelworkers engage in rent seeking when they lobby for higher subsidies, the costs of which are passed on to taxpayers or consumers.

4 The works of Adam Przeworski and colleagues cited herein are notable exceptions.
5 I discuss the various measures, their strengths and weaknesses, in greater detail
   below.
6 See Przeworski (1999) for a spirited defence of a minimalist conception.
7 Some Asian statesmen such as Lee Kuan Yew of Singapore and Mahathir
   Mohamed of Malaysia argue that Asian values (one of which is respect for
   authority), rather than Western-style liberal democracy, will best secure the
   economic futures of poor countries. As Amartya Sen points out, however, the
   determination of Asian values depends on who is asked—for example, the
   Burmese junta, or the Nobel Peace prizewinner, Aung San Suu Kyi?
8 How this comes about and exactly under what "democratic" conditions are
   still unclear, except that capital in general will suffer and labour will gain.
9 George Tsebelis (1995) pioneered the veto point framework and highlights the
   various types of democracy—presidential versus parliamentary and unicameral
   versus bicameral—that sport similar and differing types of veto points, which
   yield different outcomes. His work underscores the difficulty of precisely pin-
   pointing one or another system as being "better" in terms of outcomes, given
   partisan and institutional veto players that cut across the different types of
   systems. Some studies have explicitly used measures of democracy that seek to
   distinguish the degree of political power concentration and find favorable
   effects on growth, but these studies do not connect their measures to a theory
   of democracy; see Henisz (2000).
10 See Weede (1996b) and Wintrobe (1990) for arguments about qualitative differences among dictatorships.
11 The "median voter theory" is one of the most elegant theories explaining the
   failure of democracy in promoting economic growth. Accordingly, in a society
   with a skewed distribution, the median voter will demand redistribution at the
   expense of investment. There is little evidence, however, that inequality among
   democracies is associated with lower growth. In fact, lower levels of inequality
   seem to spur growth despite regime type, see Knack and Keefer (1997a). The
   problem for large N tests of this issue is that most societies with high inequality
   are also autocracies rather than democracies.
12 Rent-seeking activity is generally defined as the allocation of "rents" to individuals and groups through political manipulation of the market. In other
   words, these individuals and groups, through political means, acquire more
   than what the market will afford for whatever activities they may be engaged
   in. For example, producers seek rents when they lobby for subsidies.
13 Some rational choice theories assume that leaders fear being ousted when they
   perform badly and therefore the larger the winning coalition, such as in a
   majoritarian system, the greater the fear of being thrown out (Bueno de
   Mesquita *et al.*, 2000). This factor induces better performance. The problem is
   that there is little evidence for retrospective voting, largely because voters are
   not informed and incumbents obfuscate issues (Przeworski, 1999). Moreover,
   citizens' preferences are heterogeneous. To illustrate simply, if economic performance alone was to determine reelection, Al Gore should never have lost the
   2000 US presidential election! Nor is there clear evidence to suggest that
   democracies are free traders, even if most consumers benefit from free trade.
14 Henisz (2000) uses an index of political constraints, which measures the degree
   to which policy preferences could be "checked" by other veto players, and
   finds favorable effects on growth. While my arguments are similar to his as to
   why the degree of competition should matter for growth, the political constraints argument is not well connected to qualitative aspects of democracy.
15 Even populists of the right and left within established democracies make

similar claims. For an excellent explication of the tensions between democracy's "two faces," populism's "redemptive" impulse, and liberal democracy's "pragmatism," see Canovan (1999).

16 Most colonies of former Western powers adopted similar constitutions to those of the colonizer. Moreover, the nationalist elites within these countries had mobilized the masses in the cause of independence with the promise of universal suffrage.

17 Communist societies especially eulogized participation and flaunted universal suffrage as a uniquely socialist virtue. This is not to say that all "third wave" democracies are highly inclusive. Indeed, many of the Baltic states especially have excluded certain minorities from participating in politics. However, most democracies, today, insure universal suffrage almost without qualification.

18 See the excellent treatment of the subject in Przeworski *et al.* (1999).

19 David Waldner (1999) provides an excellent case-study-based, comparative analysis of how problems of state building in developing countries relate to the types of elite–mass accommodations stemming from whether or not mass mobilization coincided with state-building efforts. Where broad, cross-class coalitions were necessary, states resorted to "precocious Keynesianism." Where such coalitions were unnecessary, such as in Taiwan and Korea, then developmental states were possible.

5 Empirics of democracy and growth, and growth of democracy

1 Most analyses using the panel regression method utilize 10-year periods. Barro's panel analyses cover the periods 1965–75, 1975–85, and 1985–90. His results are consistent over these three time periods.

2 Downloaded from www.freetheworld.com/download.html.

3 Both measures of democracy exhibit positive and statistically highly significant effects if the human capital variable is left out of the model, suggesting the close link between democracy and levels of human capital beyond wealth; see also Barro (1998).

4 Some observers have argued that postmodern politics has increased the level of participation, and others that postmodern politics is inimical to growth, see Lane and Ersson (1990) and Granato *et al.* (1996). Thus, the negative effect of participation might very well be capturing a "postmodern effect" via the high degree of participation among the industrialized democracies.

5 To gauge whether the negative effect of participation on growth is a function of extreme poverty as Lipset intimates, I constructed a dummy variable for poorest countries by taking the mean income at each period and subtracting half a standard deviation (mean –½ standard deviation). Thus poor countries were those below 1,300 in 1970 (PPP$), 1,800 in 1980, and 2,400 in 1990. An interactive term of poorest country and participation proved to be positive and statistically insignificant, signifying that mass poverty alone is not the conditioning factor for the negative effect of participation on growth.

6 Hypothetically, a percentage increase in participation holding competition at the mean value for industrial democracies (58.7) will only reduce growth by −0.82 percent on average if an authoritarian regime increases participation to the level of industrial democracies.

7 The 38 missing cases are largely made up of small African countries representing the 1970–80 time period. Except for this, there is no discernible pattern to these cases that explains the result.

8 The long-run effect is the sum of coefficients of the lagged terms for the trade variable divided by 1 minus the sum of the coefficients for democracy.

9 The dummy variable for the French legal system is left out to avoid collinearity.

10 Ethnolinguistic fractionalization is the average value of 5 indices: (1) index of ethnolinguistic fractionalization in 1960, which measures the probability that two randomly selected people will not belong to the same ethnolinguistic group, (2) probability that two randomly selected people speak the same language, (3) probability that two randomly selected people do not speak the same language, (4) percentage of population not speaking the official language, and (5) percentage of population not speaking the most widely spoken language; see La Porta *et al.* (1998) for sources.

11 There is a mountain of literature on oil rents, Islam, and the problem of the democratic deficit in the Middle East. See Ross (2001) for an excellent review. Recent studies on civil war have also highlighted the corrosive impact of resource wealth that could have indirect effects on democratization (Collier and Hoeffler, 2000; de Soysa, 2002).

12 These data are from Global Development Network. Oil dependence is a discrete variable taking on the value 1 if petroleum exports are larger than 50 percent of GDP, and 0 if not. Data on religion is percentage of population that is, Muslim, Catholic, Protestant, and other; La Porta *et al.* (1998) ("other" is left out to avoid collinearity).

13 FDI's effect is considerably stronger without level of urbanization in the model, almost double the impact (results not shown).

14 Income's effect is considerably stronger without urbanization in the model (results not shown).

15 Burkhart and de Soysa (2002) report a positive effect between Protestantism and democracy but using the Polity IV index of democracy.

16 Burkhart and de Soysa (2002) report a negative effect of Islam on democracy, net of oil wealth, using the Polity IV index of democracy.

17 Trade's effect is positive and statistically highly significant when urbanization and FDI are left out of the model. Moreover, including the gravity effect by adding the size of the population had little impact on the results in the table (results not shown).

Bibliography

Abramovitz, M. (1986) "Catching Up, Forging Ahead, and Falling Behind," *Journal of Economic History* 35, 1: 386–405.

Adams, F., Gupta, S. D., and Mengisteab, K. (1999) "Globalization and the Developing World: An Introduction," in Adams, F., Gupta, S. D., and Mengisteab, K. (eds) *Globalization and the Dilemmas of the State in the South*, London: Macmillan.

Ades, A. and Di Tella, R. (1999) "Rents, Competition, and Corruption," *American Economic Review* 89, 4: 982–93.

Ahiakpor, J. C. W. (1990) *Multinationals and Economic Development: An Integration of Competing Theories*, New York: Routledge.

Aikman, D. (1986) *Pacific Rim: Area of Change, Area of Opportunity*, Boston: Little, Brown.

Alesina, A. and Perotti, R. (1994) "The Political Economy of Growth: A Critical Survey of the Literature," *World Bank Economic Review* 8, 3: 351–71.

Alesina, A., Özler, S., Roubini, N., and Swagel, P. (1992) "Political Instability and Economic Growth," *NBER Working Paper 4173*, Boston, MA: National Bureau of Economic Research

Alesina, A., Spolaore, E., and Wacziarg, R. (2000) "Economic Integration and Political Disintegration," *American Economic Review* 90, 5: 1,276–96.

Amin, S. (1990) *Maldevelopment*, London: Zed Books.

Amirahmadi, H. and Wu, W. (1994) "Foreign Direct Investment in Developing Countries," *Journal of Developing Areas* 28, January: 167–90.

Amsden, A. H. (1988) "Taiwan's Economic History: A Case of Etatisme and a Challenge of Dependency Theory," in Bates, R. H. (ed.) *Toward a Political Economy of Development*, Berkeley, CA: University of California Press.

Apodaca, C. (2001) "Global Economic Patterns and Personal Integrity Rights after the Cold War," *International Studies Quarterly* 45, 4: 587–602.

Armijo, L. E. (ed.) (1999a) *Financial Globalization and Democracy in Emerging Markets*, Basingstoke: Palgrave.

Armijo, L. E. (1999b) "Mixed Blessings: Expectations about Capital Flows and Democracy in Emerging Markets," in Armijo, L. E. (ed.) *Financial Globalization and Democracy in Emerging Markets*, Basingstoke: Palgrave.

Aron, J. (2000) "Growth and Institutions: A Review of the Evidence," *World Bank Research Observer* 15, 1: 99–135.

Arrow, K. (1962) "The Economic Implications of Learning by Doing," *Review of Economic Studies* 29: 155–79.

Baghwati, J. (1993) "Democracy and Development," in Diamond, L. and Plattner,

M. F. (eds) *Capitalism, Socialism, and Democracy Revisited*, Baltimore, MD: Johns Hopkins University Press.

Baghwati, J. (2000) *The Wind of the Hundred Days: How Washington Mismanaged Globalization*, London: MIT Press.

Baldwin, R. E. and Martin, P. (1999) "Two Waves of Globalization: Superficial Similarities, Fundamental Differences," in Siebert, H. (ed.) *Globalization and Labor*, Tübingen: Mohr Siebeck.

Baldwin, R. E. and Seghezza, E. (1996) "Trade-Induced Investment-led Growth," Cambridge, MA: National Bureau of Economic Research.

Ballmer-Cao, T. and Scheidegger, J. (1979) *Compendium of Data For World-System Analysis*, Zurich: University of Zurich.

Baran, P. (1962) *The Political Economy of Growth*, New York: Monthly Review Press.

Bardhan, P. (1993) "Symposium on Democracy and Development," *Journal of Economic Perspectives* 73: 45–9.

Barro, R. J. (1991) "Economic Growth in a Cross Section of Countries," *Quarterly Journal of Economics* 106, 2: 407–43.

Barro, R. J. (1996) "Democracy and Growth," *Journal of Economic Growth* 1: 2–27.

Barro, R. J. (1998) *Determinants of Economic Growth: A Cross-Country Empirical Study*, Cambridge, MA: MIT Press.

Barro, R. J. (2001) "Quantity and Quality of Economic Growth," Fifth Annual Conference of the Central Bank of Chile, November 29–30 2001, Santiago, Chile.

Bates, R. H. (ed.) (1988) *Toward a Political Economy of Development: A Rational Choice Perspective*, Berkeley, CA: University of California Press.

Beck, T., Clarke, G., Groff, A., Keefer, P., and Walsh, P. (2001) "New Tools in Comparative Political Economy: The Database of Political Institutions," *World Bank Economic Review* 15, 1: 165–76.

Becker, D. S., Frieden, J., Schatz, S. P., and Sklar, R. L. (1987) *Postimperialism: International Capitalism and Development in the Late Twentieth Century*, Boulder, CO: Lynne Rienner.

Becker, G. and Barro, R. (1988) "A Reformulation of the Economic Theory of Fertility," *Quarterly Journal of Economics* 103: 1–25.

Berger, P. L. (1993) "The Uncertain Triumph of Democratic Capitalism," in Diamond, L. and Plattner, M. F. (eds) *Capitalism, Socialism, and Democracy Revisited*, Baltimore, MD: Johns Hopkins University Press.

Bhagwati, J. (1966) *The Economics of Underdeveloped Countries*, New York: McGraw-Hill.

Bhagwati, J. (1999) "Globalization: Who Gains, Who Loses?" in Siebert, H. (ed.) *Globalization and Labor*, Tübingen: Mohr Siebeck.

Bienen, H. (1970) "One-Party Systems in Africa," in Huntington, S. P. and Moore, C. (eds) *Authoritarian Politics in Modern Society*, New York: Basic Books.

Binder, L. (1971) "Crises of Political Development," in Binder, L., Coleman, J., LaPalombara, J., Pye, L., Verba, S., and Weiner, M. (eds) *Crises and Sequences in Political Development*, Princeton, NJ: Princeton University Press.

Birdsall, N. and Lawrence, R. Z. (1999) "Deep Integration and Trade Agreements: Good for Developing Countries?" in Kaul, I., Grunberg, I., and Stern, M. (eds) *Global Public Goods: International Cooperation in the 21st Century*, Oxford: Oxford University Press.

Blomström, M., Lipsey, R. E., and Zejan, M. (1992) "What Explains Developing Country Growth?" Cambridge, MA: National Bureau of Economic Research.

Bollen, K. A. (1983) "World System Position, Dependency, and Democracy: The Cross-National Evidence," *American Sociological Review* 48: 468–79.

Bollen, K. A. (1988) "If You Ignore Outliers Will They Go Away?: A Reply to Gasiorowski," *Comparative Political Studies* 20, 4: 516–22.

Bollen, K. A. (1993) "Liberal Democracy: Validity and Method Factors in Cross-National Measures," *American Journal of Political Science* 37: 1,207–30.

Bordo, M. D., Eichengreen, B., and Irwin, D. A. (1999) "Is Globalization Today Really Different Than Globalization a Hundred Years Ago?" Cambridge, MA: National Bureau of Economic Reasearch.

Borenzstein, E., de Gregorio, J., and Lee, J. (1998) "How Does Foreign Investment Affect Economic Growth?" *Journal of International Economics* 45: 115–35.

Bornschier, V. (1980) "Multinational Corporations and Economic Growth: A Cross-National Test of the Decapitalization Thesis," *Journal of Development Economics* 7: 191–210.

Bornschier, V. and Chase-Dunn, C. (1985) *Transnational Corporations and Underdevelopment*, New York: Praeger.

Boswell, T. and Dixon, W. (1990) "Dependency and Rebellion: A Cross-National Analysis," *American Sociological Review* 55: 540–59.

Boutros-Ghali, B. (1995) *An Agenda for Development*, New York: United Nations.

Bradshaw, Y. W. (1988) "Reassessing Economic Dependency and Uneven Development: The Kenyan Experience," *American Sociological Review* 53: 693–708.

Brecher, J. and Costello, T. (1994) *Global Village or Global Pillage: Economic Reconstruction from the Bottom up*, Boston: South End Press.

Browett, J. (1985) "The Newly Industrializing Countries and the Radical Theories of Development," *World Development* 13, 7: 789–809.

Brunetti, A. (1997) "Politics and Economic Growth: A Cross-Country Data Perspective," Paris: OECD.

Bueno de Mesquita, B., Morrow, J. D., Siverson, R. M., and Smith, A. (2000) "Political Institutions, Political Survival, and Policy Success," in Bueno de Mesquita, B. and Root, H. L. (eds) *Governing for Prosperity*, New Haven, CT: Yale University Press.

Bueno de Mesquita, B. and Root, H. L. (2000) "When Bad Economics Is Good Politics," in Bueno de Mesquita, B. and Root, H. L. (eds) *Governing for Prosperity*, New Haven, CT: Yale University Press.

Burkhart, R. E. and de Soysa, I. (2002) "Open Borders, Open Regimes? FDI, Trade, and Democratization, 1970–1999," Bonn: Center for Development Research (ZEF).

Burkhart, R. E. and Lewis-Beck, M. S. (1994) "Comparative Democracy: The Economic Development Thesis," *American Political Science Review* 88, 4: 903–10.

Burtless, G., Lawrence, R. Z., and Shapiro, R. (1998) *Globaphobia: Confronting Fears About Open Trade*, Washington, DC: Brookings Institute Press.

Cairncross, F. (2001) *The Death of Distance: How the Communications Revolution Is Changing our Lives*, Cambridge, MA: Harvard Business School Press.

Cammack, P., Pool, D., and Tordoff, W. (1993) *Third World Politics: A Comparative Introduction*, Baltimore, MD: Johns Hopkins University Press.

Canovan, M. (1999) "Trust the People! Populism and the Two Faces of Democracy," *Political Studies* 40, 7: 2–16.

Cardoso, E. and Fishlow, A. (1992) "Latin American Economic Development: 1950–1980," *Journal of Latin American Studies* 24: 197–218.

Cardoso, F. H. and Faletto, E. (1979) *Dependency and Development in Latin America*, Berkeley, CA: University of California Press.

Caves, R. E. (1982) *Multinational Enterprise and Economic Analysis*, New York: Cambridge University Press.

Chen, S. and Ravallion, M. (1998) "How Did the World's Poorest Fare in the 1990s?" Washington, DC: World Bank.

Collier, D. and Levitsky, S. (1997) "Democracy with Adjectives: Conceptual Innovation in Comparative Research," *World Politics* 49, April: 430–51.

Collier, P. and Gunning, J. W. (1999) "Explaining African Economic Performance," *Journal of Economic Literature* 37: 64–111.

Collier, P. and Hoeffler, A. (2000) "Greed and Grievance in Civil War," Washington, DC: World Bank, Development Research Group.

Crepaz, M. (1996) "Constitutional Structures and Regime Performance in 18 Industrialized Democracies: A Test of Olson's Hypothesis," *European Journal of Political Research* 29: 87–104.

Cross, P. (1995) "Cuba's Socialist Revolution: Last Rites or Rejuvenation?" in Gills, B. and Qadir, S. (eds) *Regimes in Crisis: The Post-Soviet Era and the Implications for Development*, London: Zed Books.

Dahl, R. A. (1971) *Polyarchy: Participation and Opposition*, New Haven, CT: Yale University Press.

Dahl, R. A. (1985) *A Preface to Economic Democracy*, Berkeley, CA: University of California Press.

Dahl, R. A. (2000) *On Democracy*, New Haven, CT: Yale University Press.

de Melo, L. R. J. (1999) "Foreign Direct Investment-Led Growth: Evidence From Time Series and Panel Data," *Oxford Economic Papers* 51, 1: 133–51.

de Soysa, I. (2002) "Paradise is a Bazaar? Greed, Creed, and Governance in Civil War, 1989–1999," *Journal of Peace Research* 39, 4: 395–416.

de Soysa, I. and Oneal, J. R. (1999) "Boon or Bane? Reassessing the Productivity of Foreign Direct Investment," *American Sociological Review* 64, October: 766–82.

Deininger, K. and Squire, L. (1997) "A New Data Set Measuring Income Inequality," *The World Bank Economic Review* 10: 565–91.

DeLong, J. Bradford (1988) "Productivity Growth, Convergence, and Welfare: Comment," *American Economic Review* 78, 1: 138–54.

DeLong, J. Bradford (2000) "The Economic History of the Twentieth Century: Slouching Towards Utopia?" Berkeley, CA: Department of Economics, University of California, Berkeley.

Dethier, J.-J. (1999) "Governance and Economic Performance: A Survey," Bonn: Center for Development Research, ZEF.

DFID, UK government (2000) "Eliminating World Poverty: Making Globalization Work for the Poor," London: Department for International Development (DFID).

Diamond, L. (1996) "Is the Third Wave Over?" *Journal of Democracy* 7, 3: 20–37.

Diamond, L., Linz, J., and Lipset, S. M. (eds) (1995) *Politics in Developing Countries: Comparing Experiences with Democracy*, Boulder, CO: Lynne Rienner.

Diamond, L. and Plattner, M. F. (eds) (1993) *Capitalism, Socialism, and Democracy Revisited*, London: Johns Hopkins University Press.

Diamond, L. and Plattner, M. F. (eds) (1994) *Nationalism, Ethnic Conflict, and Democracy*, Baltimore, MD: Johns Hopkins University Press.

Dix, R. H. (1994) "History and Democracy Revisited," *Comparative Politics* 27, 1: 94–105.

Dixon, W. and Boswell, T. (1996a) "Dependency, Disarticulation, and Denominator Effects: Another Look at Foreign Capital Penetration," *American Journal of Sociology* 102, 2: 576–784.

Dixon, W. and Boswell, T. (1996b) "Differential Productivity, Negative Externalities, and Foreign Capital Dependency: A Reply to Firebaugh," *American Journal of Sociology* 102, 2: 576–784.

Dollar, D. and Kraay, A. (2000) "Growth *Is* Good for the Poor," Washington, DC: World Bank.

Dos Santos, T. (1970) "The Structure of Dependence," *American Economic Review* 60: 231–6.

Dunning, J. H. (1992) "Governments, Markets, and Multinational Enterprises: Some Emerging Issues," *International Trade Journal* 7, fall: 111–29.

Dunning, J. H. (2001) *Global Capitalism at Bay?* London: Routledge.

Dunning, J. H. and Hamdani, K. A. (1997) *The New Globalism and Developing Countries*, New York: United Nations University Press.

Easterly, W. and Sewadeh, M. (2001) "Global Development Network Growth Database," Washington, DC: World Bank.

Eckstein, H. (1996) "Lessons for the 'Third Wave' from the First: An Essay on Democratization," Irvine, CA: Center for the Study of Democracy, University of California Irvine.

Eder, M. (1994) "Economic Democracy: What Can the Intellectuals Do?" in Soemardjan, S. and Thompson, K. W. (eds) *Culture Development and Democracy: The Role of the Intellectual*, New York: United Nations University Press.

Elster, J., Offe, C., and Preuss, U. K. (1998) *Rebuilding the Ship at Sea: Institutional Design in Post-Communist Societies*, Cambridge: Cambridge University Press.

Emmanuel, A. (1969) *Unequal Exchange: A Study of the Imperialism of Trade*, New York: Monthly Review Press.

Evans, P. B. (1979) *Dependent Development: The Alliance of Multinational, State, and Local Capital in Brazil*, Princeton, NJ: Princeton University Press.

Falk, R. (1999) *Predatory Globalization: A Critique*, Cambridge: Polity Press.

Firebaugh, G. (1992) "Growth Effects of Foreign and Domestic Investment," *American Journal of Sociology* 98, 1: 105–30.

Firebaugh, G. (1996) "Does Foreign Capital Harm Poor Nations? New Estimates Based on Dixon and Boswell's Measures of Capital Penetration," *American Journal of Sociology* 102, 2: 563–78.

Frank, A. G. (1969) *Capitalism and Underdevelopment in Latin America*, New York: Monthly Review Press.

Frankel, J. A. (2000) "Globalization of the Economy," in Nye, J. S. and Donahue, J. D. (eds) *Governance in a Globalizing World*, Cambridge, MA, and Washington, DC: Visions of Governance for the 21st Century and Brookings Institute Press.

Frankel, J. A. and Romer, D. (1999) "Does Trade Cause Growth?" *American Economic Review* 89, 3: 379–99.

Freedom House (2002) "Annual Survey of Freedom Country Scores 1972–73 to

1999–2000," Freedom House, April 18, http://www.freedomhouse.org/ratings/index.htm

Frey, B., Pommerrehne, W. W., Schneider, F., and Guy, G. (1984) "Consensus and Dissention Among Economists: An Empirical Inquiry," *American Economic Review, Papers and Proceedings* 74: 986–94.

Fukuyama, F. (1991) *The End of History and the Last Man*, Oxford: Oxford University Press.

Galtung, J. (1971) "A Structural Theory of Imperialism," *Journal of Peace Research* 8, 2: 81–117.

Gasiorowski, M. J. (1988) "Economic Dependence and Political Democracy: A Cross-National Study," *Comparative Political Studies* 20, 4: 489–515.

Gasiorowski, M. J. (1996) "An Overview of the Political Regime Change Dataset," *Comparative Political Studies* 29, 4: 469–83.

Gasiorowski, M. J. and Power, T. J. (1998) "The Structural Determinants of Democratic Consolidation: Evidence from the Third World," *Comparative Political Studies* 31, 6: 740–71.

Gatti, R. (1999) "Explaining Corruption: Are Open Countries Less Corrupt?" Washington, DC: World Bank.

Gereffi, G. (1985) "The Renegotiation of Dependency and the Limits of State Autonomy in Mexico (1975–1982)," in Moran, T. H. (ed.) *Multinational Corporations: The Political Economy of Foreign Direct Investment*, Lexington, MA: Lexington Books.

Gerschenkron, A. (1962) *Economic Backwardness in Historical Perspective*, Cambridge, MA: Harvard University Press.

Giddens, A. (1999) *Runaway World: How Globalization Is Reshaping our Lives*, London: Profile Books.

Gill, S. (1995) "Theorizing the Interregnum: The Double Movement and Global Politics in the 1990s," in Hettne, B. (ed.) *International Political Economy: Understanding Global Disorder*, London: Zed Books.

Gill, S. (1997) "Globalization, Democratization, and the Politics of Indifference," in Mittelman, J. (ed.) *Globalization: Critical Reflections*, Boulder, CO: Lynne Rienner.

Gills, B. K. (2002) "Democratizing Globalization and Globalizing Democracy," *Annals of the American Academy of Political and Social Science* 581, May: 158–71.

Gills, B. K. and Qadir, S. (eds) (1995) *Regimes in Crisis: The Post-Soviet Era and the Implications for Development*, London: Zed Books.

Gilpin, R. (1976) "The Political Economy of the Multinational Corporation," *American Political Science Review* 70: 184–91.

Gilpin, R. (1981) *War and Change in World Politics*, Cambridge: Cambridge University Press.

Gilpin, R. (1987) *The Political Economy of International Relations*, Princeton, NJ: Princeton University Press.

Gilpin, R. (2000) *The Challenge of Global Capitalism: The World Economy in the 21st Century*, Princeton, NJ: Princeton University Press.

Gourevitch, P. (1993) "Democracy and Economic Policy: Elective Affinities and Circumstantial Conjectures," *World Development* 21, 8: 1,271–80.

Graham, E. M. (2000) *Fighting the Wrong Enemy: Antiglobal Activists and Multinational Enterprises*, Washington, DC: Institute for International Economics.

Granato, J., Inglehart, R., and Leblang, D. (1996) "The Effects of Cultural Values on Economic Development: Theory, Hypotheses, and Some Empirical Tests," *American Journal of Political Science* 40, 3: 607–31.

Granger, C. W. (1969) "Investigating Causal Relations by Econometric Models and Cross-Spectral Methods," *Econometrica* 37: 424–38.

Granger, C. W. (1988) "Some Recent Developments in a Concept of Causality," *Journal of Econometrics* 39: 7–21.

Gray, John (1999) *False Dawn: The Delusion of Global Capitalism*, London: Granta.

Grieco, J. M. (1985) "India's Experience with the International Computer Industry," in Moran, T. H. (ed.) *Multinational Corporations: The Political Economy of Foreign Direct Investment*, Lexington, MA: D. C. Heath.

Grossman, G. and Helpman, E. (1992) "Protection for Sale," *American Economic Review* 84, 4: 833–50.

Grossman, G. and Helpman, E. (1994) "Endogenous Innovation in the Theory of Growth," *Journal of Economic Perspectives* 8, 1: 23–44.

Gurr, T. R. and Jaggers, K. (1995) "Tracking Democracy's Third Wave with the Polity III Data," *Journal of Peace Research* 32, 4: 469–82.

Gwartney, J., Lawson, R., Park, W., and Skipton, C. (2001) *Economic Freedom of the World 2001: Annual Report*, Vancouver: Fraser Institute.

Haggard, S. (1990) *Pathways From the Periphery*, New York: Oxford University Press.

Haggard, S. (1997) "Democratic Institutions, Economic Policy, and Development," in Clague, C. (ed.) *Institutions and Economic Development: Growth and Governance in Less-Developed and Post-Socialist Countries*, Baltimore, MD: Johns Hopkins University Press.

Haggard, S. and Kaufman, R. R. (eds) (1992) *The Politics of Economic Adjustment*, Princeton, NJ: Princeton University Press.

Harrison, L. E. (1985) *Underdevelopment Is a State of Mind: The Latin American Case*, Cambridge, MA: Center for International Studies, Harvard University.

Harrison, L. E. and Huntington, S. P. (eds) (2000) *Culture Matters: How Values Shape Human Progress*, New York: Basic Books.

Held, D. (1995) *Democracy and the Global Order: From the Modern State to Cosmopolitan Governance*, Stanford, CA: Stanford University Press.

Held, D. and McGrew, A. (eds) (2000) *The Global Transformations Literature: An Introduction to the Globalization Debate*, Cambridge: Polity Press.

Henderson, D. (2000) "Anti-Liberalism 2000: The Rise of New Millennium Collectivism," London: Institute of Economic Affairs (IEA).

Henisz, W. J. (2000) "The Institutional Environment for Economic Growth," *Economics and Politics* 12, 1: 1–31.

Hettne, B. (1995) *International Political Economy: Understanding Global Disorder*, London: Zed Books.

Hettne, B. (2002) "In Search of World Order," in Hettne, B. and Odén, B. (eds) *Global Governance in the 21st Century: Alternative Perspectives on World Order*, Stockholm: Almkvist and Wicksell.

Hoffmann, S. (2002) "Clash of Globalizations," *Foreign Affairs* 81, 4: 104–15.

Holmes, S. (1995) *Passions and Constraints: On the Theory of Liberal Democracy*, Chicago: University of Chicago Press.

Hoogvelt, A. (2001) *Globalization and the Postcolonial World: The New Political Economy of Development*, Basingstoke: Palgrave.

Huntington, S. P. (1968) *Poitical Order in Changing Societies*, New York: Yale University Press.

Huntington, S. P. (1991) *The Third Wave*, Norman, OK: University of Oklahoma Press.

Huntington, S. P. and Dominguez, Jorge (1975) "Political Development," in Greenstein, Fred and Polsby, Nelson (eds) *Handbook of Political Science*, vol. iii, Reading, MA: Addison-Wesley.

Huntington, S. P. and Nelson, J. (1976) *No Easy Choice: Political Participation in Developing Countries*, Cambridge, MA: Harvard University Press.

Hymer, S. (1972) "The Multinational Corporation and the Law of Uneven Development," in Bhagwati, J. N. (ed.) *Economics and the World Order*, New York: Macmillan.

IMF (2000) "Globalization: Threat or Opportunity?" Washington, DC: International Monetary Fund (IMF).

Jackman, R. W. (1982) "Dependence on Foreign Investment and Economic Growth in the Third World," *World Politics* 34: 175–96.

Jenkins, J. C. and Schock, K. (1992) "Global Structures and Political Processes in the Study of Domestic Political Conflict," *Annual Review of Sociology* 18: 161–85.

Karl, T. L. (1997) *The Paradox of Plenty: Oil Booms and Petro-States*, Berkeley, CA: University of California Press.

Kaufmann, Daniel, Kraay, Art and Zoido-Lobaton, Pablo (1999) "Governance Matters," World Bank policy research paper #2196, Washington, DC: World Bank.

Keech, William R. (1995) *Economic Politics: The Costs of Democracy*, Cambridge: Cambridge University Press.

Kentor, J. (1998) "The Long Term Effects of Foreign Capital Penetration on Economic Growth, 1940–1990," *American Journal of Sociology* 103, 4: 1,024–46.

Keohane, R. O. and Nye, J. S. (2000) "Introduction," in Nye, J. S. and Donahue, J. D. (eds) *Governance in a Globalizing World*, Cambridge, MA, and Washington, DC: Visions of Governance for the 21st Century and Brookings Institute Press.

Kindleberger, C. P. (1975) "The Rise of Free Trade in Western Europe," *Journal of Economic History* 35: 1.

King, G., Keohane, R., and Verba, S. (1994) *Designing Social Inquiry: Scientific Inference from Qualitative Research*, Princeton, NJ: Princeton University Press.

Knack, S. and Keefer, P. (1997a) "Does Income Inequality Harm Growth Only in Democracies? A Replication and Extension," *American Journal of Political Science* 41, 1: 323–32.

Knack, S. and Keefer, P. (1997b) "Does Social Capital Have an Economic Payoff? A Cross-Country Investigation," paper presented at the annual meeting of the American Political Science Association, Washington, DC.

Kobrin, S. J. (1976) "Foreign Direct Investment, Industrialization, and Social Change," *Journal of Conflict Resolution* 20, 3: 497–522.

Korany, B. (1994) "End of History, or its Continuation and Accentuation? The Global South and the 'New Transformation' Literature," *Third World Quarterly* 15, 1: 7–15.

Kornhauser, W. (1959) *The Politics of Mass Society*, London: Routledge and Kegan Paul.

Korten, D. C. (2001) *When Corporations Rule the World*, Bloomfield, CT: Kumarian.

Krasner, S. D. (1985) *Structural Conflict: The Third World Against Global Liberalism*, Berkeley, CA: University of California Press.

Krugman, P. and Venables, A. J. (1995) "Globalization and the Inequality of Nations," *Quarterly Journal of Economics* 110, 4: 857–80.

Kuznets, S. (1966) *Modern Economic Growth: Rate, Structure, and Spread*, New Haven, CT: Yale University Press.

La Porta, R., Lopez-de-Silanes, F., Schleifer, A., and Vishny, R. (1998) *The Quality of Government*, Cambridge, MA: National Bureau of Economic Research.

Laitin, D. D. (2000) "Comparative Politics: The State of the Subdiscipline," paper presented at the annual meeting of the American Political Science Association, Washington, DC.

Lal, D. and Myint, H. (1996) *The Political Economy of Poverty, Equity, and Growth*, Oxford: Clarendon Press.

Lall, S. and Streeten, P. (1977) *Foreign Investment, Transnationals and Developing Countries*, Boulder, CO: Westview Press.

Lane, J.-E. and Ersson, S. (1986) "Political Institutions, Public Policy and Economic Growth," *Scandinavian Political Studies* 9, 1: 19–33.

Lane, J.-E. and Ersson, S. (1990) "Macro and Micro Understanding in Political Science: What Explains Electoral Participation?" *European Journal of Political Research* 18, 4: 457–65.

Lane, J.-E. and Ersson, S. (1994) *Comparative Politics: An Introduction and New Approach*, Cambridge: Polity Press.

Lane, P. R. and Milesi-Ferretti, G. M. (2000) "The External Wealth of Nations: Measures of Foreign Assets and Liabilities for Industrial and Developing Countries," Washington, DC: International Monetary Fund (IMF).

Leblang, D. (1996) "Property Rights, Democracy and Economic Growth," *Political Research Quarterly* 49, 1: 5–26.

Leblang, David (1997), "Political Democracy and Economic Growth: Pooled Cross-Sectional and Time Series Evidence," *British Journal of Political Science*, 27: 453–72.

Leftwich, A. (1995) "Model of the Developmental State," *Journal of Development Studies* 31, 3: 400–27.

Lele, U. and Nabi, I. (1991) "Aid, Capital Flows and Development: A Synthesis," in Lele, U. and Nabi, I. (eds) *Transitions in Development: The Role of Aid and Commercial Flows*, San Francisco: An International Centre for Economic Growth Publication.

Levine, R. and Renelt, D. (1992) "A Sensitivity Analysis of Cross-Country Growth Regressions," *American Economic Review* 82, 4: 942–63.

Lewis-Beck, M. S. (1988) *Economics and Elections: The Major Western Democracies*, Ann Arbor, MI: University of Michigan Press.

Lijphart, A. (1977) *Democracy in Plural Societies: A Comparative Exploration*, New Haven, CT: Yale University Press.

Lijphart, A. (1984) *Democracies: Patterns of Majoritarian and Consensus Government in Twenty-One Countries*, New Haven, CT: Yale University Press.

Lijphart, A. (1993) "Constitutional Choices for New Democracies," in Diamond, L.

and Plattner, M. (eds) *The Global Resurgence of Democracy*, Baltimore, MD: Johns Hopkins University Press.

Lijphart, A. (1999) *Patterns of Democracy*, New Haven, CT: Yale University Press.

Lipset, S. M. (1959) "Some Social Requisites of Democracy: Economic Development and Political Legitimacy," *American Political Science Review* 53: 69–105.

Lomborg, B. (2001) *The Skeptical Environmentalist: Measuring the Real State of the World*, Cambridge: Cambridge University Press.

London, B. (1988) "Dependence, Distorted Development, and Fertility Trends in Non-Core Nations: A Structural Analysis of Cross-National Data," *American Sociological Review* 53: 606–18.

London, B. and Williams, B. (1988) "Multinational Corporate Penetration, Protest, and Basic Needs Provision in Non-Core Nations: A Cross-National Analysis," *Social Forces* 66: 747–73.

Lucas, R. E. (1988) "On the Mechanics of Economic Development," *Journal of Monetary Economics* 22: 3–42.

Lucas, R. E. (1990) "Why Doesn't Capital Flow from Rich to Poor Countries?" *American Economic Association Papers and Proceedings* 80, 2: 92–102.

Maddison, A. (1989) *The World Economy in the 20th Century*, Washington, DC: OECD Publications.

Mahdavi, S. and Sohrabian, A. (1991) "The Link Between the Rate of Growth of Stock Prices and the Rate of Growth of GNP in the United States: A Granger Causality Test," *American Economist* 35, 2: 41–8.

Mankiw, G., Romer, D., and Weil, D. (1992) "A Contribution to the Empirics of Economic Growth," *Quarterly Journal of Economics* 107, 2: 407–37.

Mansfield, E., Milner, H., and Rosendorff, P. B. (2001) "Why Democracies Cooperate More: Electoral Control and International Trade Agreements," paper presented at the Fourth Pan-European International Relations Conference, September 6–10, University of Kent, Canterbury.

Martin, H.-P. and Schumann, H. (1997) *The Global Trap: Globalization and the Assault on Democracy and Prosperity*, London: Zed Books.

Marx, K. and Engels, F. (1972) "The Communist Manifesto," in Tucker, R. C. (ed.) *The Marx–Engels Reader*, New York: W. W. Norton.

McClelland, D. C. (1961) *The Achieving Society*, Princeton, NJ: Van Nostrand.

McDonald, S. and Roberts, J. (2002) "Growth and Multiple Forms of Human Capital in an Augmented Solow Model: A Panel Data Investigation," *Economic Letters* 74: 271–6.

Mehta, L., Leach, M., Newell, P., Scoones, I., Sivaramakrishnan, K., and Way, S.-A. (1999) "Exploring Understandings of Institutions and Uncertainty: New Directions in Natural Resource Management," Brighton: Institute of Development Studies (IDS), University of Sussex.

Melchior, A., Telle, K., and Wiig, H. (2000) "Globalization and Inequality: World Income Distribution and Living Standards, 1960–1998," Oslo: Royal Norwegian Ministry of Foreign Affairs.

Menon, R. and Oneal, J. R. (1986) "Explaining Imperialism: The State of the Art as Reflected in Three Theories," *Polity* 19, 2: 169.

Micklethwait, J. and Wooldridge, A. (2000) *A Future Perfect: The Challenge and Hidden Promise of Globalization*, New York: Crown.

Milanovic, B. (2001) "World Income Inequality in the Second Half of the 20th Century," Washington, DC: World Bank.

Milner, H. and Keohane, R. O. (1996) "Internationalization and Domestic Politics: An Introduction," in Milner, H. and Keohane, R. O. (eds) *Internationalization and Domestic Politics*, Cambridge: Cambridge University Press.

Milner, H. and Kubota, K. (2001) "Why the Rush to Free Trade? Democracy and Trade Policy in the Developing World," Annual Meeting of the American Political Science Association, August 30–September 2, San Francisco, CA.

Mittelman, J. H. (2000) *The Globalization Syndrome: Transformation and Resistance*, Princeton, NJ: Princeton University Press.

Mittelman, J. H. (ed.) (1997) *Globalization: Critical Reflections*, Boulder, CO: Lynne Rienner.

Miyoshi, M. (1993) "A Borderless World? From Colonialism to Transnationalism and the Decline of the Nation-State," *Critical Inquiry* 19, summer: 726–51.

Moe, T. M. and Caldwell, M. (1994) "The Institutional Foundations of Democratic Government: A Comparison of Presidential and Parliamentary Systems," *Journal of Institutional and Theoretical Economics* 150, 1: 171–95.

Moran, T. H. (ed.) (1985) *Multinational Corporations: The Political Economy of Foreign Direct Investment*, Lexington, MA: Lexington Books.

Mueller, J. (1995) *The Quiet Cataclysm: Reflections on the Recent Transformation of World Politics*, New York: HarperCollins.

Munck, R. (2002) "Globalization and Democracy: A New 'Great Transformation'?" *Annals of the American Academy of Political and Social Science* 581, May: 10–21.

Munck, R. and Gills, B. K. (2002) "Globalization and Democracy," *The Annals of the American Academy of Political and Social Science* 581, May: 1–9.

Myrdal, Gunnar (1971) *Economic Theory and Underdeveloped Regions*, New York: Harper and Row.

Naqvi, S. N. H. (1996) "The Significance of Development Economics," *World Development* 24, 6: 975–87.

Nelson, J. M. (1987) "Political Participation," in Weiner, M. and Huntington, S. P. (eds) *Understanding Political Development*, Boston: Little, Brown.

Nhandan (1989) "Nguyen Co Thach on 1988 Events, Plans Future," *Nhandan*, Hanoi, January 1.

North, D. C. (1989) "Institutions and Economic Growth: An Historical Introduction," *World Development* 17, 9: 1,319–32.

North, D. C. (1990) *Institutions, Institutional Change and Economic Performance*, Cambridge: Cambridge University Press.

North, D. C. and Weingast, B. (1989) "Constitutions and Commitment: The Evolution of Institutions Governing Public Choice in Seventeenth-Century England," *Journal of Economic History* 49, 4: 803–32.

Nye, J. S. and Donahue, J. D. (eds) (2000) *Governance in a Globalizing World*, Cambridge, MA, and Washington, DC: Visions of Governance for the 21st Century and Brookings Institute Press.

O'Donnell, G. (1973) *Modernization and Bureaucratic Authoritarianism: Studies in Latin American Politics*, Berkeley, CA: University of California Press.

O'Donnell, G. (1995) "On the State, Democratization and Some Conceptual Problems: A Latin American View with Glances at Some Postcommunist Countries," *World Development* 21, 18: 1,355–69.

O'Donnell, G., Schmitter, P. C., and Whitehead, L. (eds) (1986) *Transitions from Authoritarian Rule*, Baltimore, MD: Johns Hopkins University Press.

Olson, M. (1965) *The Logic of Collective Action*, Cambridge, MA: Harvard University Press.

Olson, M. (1982) *The Rise and Decline of Nations: Economic Growth, Stagflation, and Social Rigidities*, New Haven, CT: Yale University Press.

Olson, M. (1993) "Dictatorship, Democracy, and Development," *American Political Science Review* 87, 3: 567–75.

Olson, M. (1996) "Big Bills Left on the Side Walk: Why Some Nations are Rich, and Others Poor," *Journal of Economic Perspectives* 10, 2: 1–24.

Oneal, J. R. (1988) "Foreign Direct Investment in Less Developed Regions," *Political Science Quarterly* 103, 1: 131–48.

Oneal, J. R. (1994) "The Affinity of Foreign Investors for Authoritarian Regimes," *Political Research Quarterly* 47: 565–88.

O'Rourke, K. H. (2001) "Globalization and Inequality: Historical Trends," paper presented at annual bank conference on Development Economics, World Bank.

O'Rourke, K. H. and Williamson, J. G. (1999) *Globalization and History: The Evolution of a Nineteenth-Century Atlantic Economy*, London: MIT Press.

Oseghale, B. D. (1993) *Political Instability, Interstate Conflict, Adverse Changes in Host Government Policies and Foreign Direct Investment: A Sensitivity Analysis*, New York: Garland.

Palma, G. (1995) "Underdevelopment and Marxism: From Marx to the Theories of Imperialism and Dependency," in Ayers, R. (ed.) *Development Studies*, Greenwich: Greenwich University Press.

Penubarti, M. and Ward, M. D. (2000) "Commerce and Democracy," June 24 2002, www.csss.washington.edu/papers/wp6.pdf

Pfaff, W. (2001) "The Business of Business Isn't Principally the Common Good," *International Herald Tribune*, January 26.

Pomeranz, K. and Topik, S. (1998) *The World That Trade Created: Society, Culture, and the World Economy, 1400–The Present*, New York: M. E. Sharp.

Powell, B. J. (2000) *Elections as Instruments of Democracy: Majoritarian and Proportional Visions*, New Haven, CT: Yale University Press.

Pritchett, L. (1997) "Divergence, Big Time," *Journal of Economic Perspectives* 11, summer: 3–17.

Przeworski, A. (1991) *Democracy and the Market: Political and Economic Reforms in Eastern Europe and Latin America*, Cambridge: Cambridge University Press.

Przeworski, A. (1999) "Minimalist Conception of Democracy: A Defense," in Shapiro, I. and Hacker-Cordón, C. (eds) *Democracy's Value*, Cambridge: Cambridge University Press.

Przeworski, A., Alvarez, M. E., Cheibub, A. J., and Limongi, F. (2000) *Democracy and Development: Political Institutions and Well-Being in the World, 1950–1990*, Cambridge: Cambridge University Press.

Przeworski, A. and Limongi, F. (1993) "Political Regimes and Economic Growth," *Journal of Economic Perspectives* 7, 3: 51–79.

Przeworski, A. and Limongi, F. (1997) "Modernization: Theories and Facts," *World Politics* 49, 1: 155–83.

Przeworski, A., Stokes, S. C., and Manin, B. (eds) (1999) *Democracy, Accountability, and Representation*, London: Cambridge University Press.

Putnam, R. (1993) *Making Democracy Work: Civic Traditions in Modern Italy*, Princeton, NJ: Princeton University Press.

Remmer, K. L. (1997) "Theoretical Decay and Theoretical Development: The Resurgence of Institutional Analysis," *World Politics* 50, October: 34–61.

Rich, B. (1995) *Mortgaging the Earth: The World Bank, Environmental Impoverishment, and the Crisis of Development*, Bellbrook Park, MA: Beacon.

Richards, D. L., Gelleny, R. D., and Sacko, D. H. (2001) "Money with a Mean Streak? Foreign Economic Penetration and Government Respect for Human Rights in Developing Countries," *International Studies Quarterly* 45, 2: 219–39.

Rodrik, D. (1997) *Has Globalization Gone too Far?* Washington, DC: Institute for International Economics.

Rodrik, D. (1998) "The Rush to Free Trade in the Developing World: Why So Late? Why Now? Will it Last?" in Sturzenegger, F. and Tommasi, M. (eds) *The Political Economy of Reform*, Cambridge, MA: MIT Press.

Rodrik, D. (1999) "Institutions for High-Quality Growth: What They Are and How to Acquire Them," paper presented at IMF conference on second-generation reforms, November 8–9, Washington, DC.

Romer, P. M. (1986) "Increasing Returns and Long-Run Growth," *Journal of Political Economy* 94, 1,002–37.

Romer, P. M. (1993) "Idea Gaps and Object Gaps in Economic Development," *Journal of Monetary Economics* 32: 543–73.

Ross, M. L. (2001) "Does Oil Hinder Democracy?" *World Politics* 53: 325–61.

Rostow, W. W. (1960) *The Stages of Economic Growth*, New York: Cambridge University Press.

Rothgeb, J. M. J. (1996) *Foreign Investment and Political Conflict in Developing Countries*, London: Praeger.

Russett, B. and Oneal, J. (2000) *Triangulating Peace: Democracy, Interdependence, and International Organizations*, London: W. W. Norton.

Sachs, J. D. and Warner, A. (1995a) "Economic Reform and the Process of Global Integration," *Brookings Papers on Economic Activity* 1: 1–117.

Sachs, J. D. and Warner, A. (1995b) "Natural Resource Abundance and Economic Growth," Cambridge, MA: National Bureau of Economic Research.

Sachs, J. D. and Warner, A. (2001) "Natural Resources and Economic Development: The Curse of Natural Resources," *European Economic Review* 45: 827–38.

Sakamoto, Y. (ed.) (1994) *Global Transformation: Challenges to the State System*, New York: United Nations University Press.

Salamon, L. M. (1994) "The Rise of the Nonprofit Sector," *Foreign Affairs* 73, 4: 109–22.

Sandoltz, W. and Koetzle, W. (2000) "Accounting for Corruption: Economic Structure, Democracy, and Trade," *International Studies Quarterly* 44, 5: 31–50.

Schneider, F. and Frey, B. (1985) "Economic and Political Determinants of Foreign Direct Investment," *World Development* 13, February: 161–80.

Schneider, G., Barbieri, K., and Gleditsch, N. P. (eds) (2003) *Globalization and Armed Conflict*, Oxford: Rowman and Littlefield.

Schumpeter, J. A. (1943) *Capitalism, Socialism and Democracy*, London: Allen and Unwin.

Seligson, M. and Passé-Smith, J. T. (eds) (1998) *Development and Underdevelopment: The Political Economy of Global Inequality*, Boulder, CO: Lynne Rienner.

Sen, A. (1999) *Development as Freedom*, New York: Alfred A. Knopf.

Sirowy, L. and Inkeles, A. (1991) "The Effects of Democracy on Economic Growth: A Review," in Sirowy, L. and Inkeles, A. (eds) *On Measuring Democracy: Its Consequences and Concomitants*, New Brunswick, NJ: Transaction Publishers.

Sklair, L. (2002) "Democracy and the Transnational Capitalist Class," *Annals of the American Academy of Political and Social Science* 581, May: 144–57.

Solow, R. M. (1956) "A Contribution to the Theory of Economic Growth," *Quarterly Journal of Economics* 70: 65–94.

Spero, J. E. (1990) *The Politics of International Economic Relations*, New York: St. Martin's.

Srinivasan, T. N. and Baghwati, J. (1999) "Outward-Orientation and Development: Are Revisionists Right?" New Haven, CT, and New York: Yale University Press and Columbia University Press.

Stata (1999) *Stata Manual Release 6*, College Station, TX: Stata Press.

Stepan, A. (1978) *The State and Society: Peru in Comparative Perspective*, Princeton, NJ: Princeton University Press.

Stiglitz, J. E. (2002) *Globalization and its Discontents*, London: W. W. Norton.

Tavares, J. (1998) "Trade Openness, Factor Proportions and Politics: An Empirical Investigation," Cambridge, MA: Harvard University Press.

Tavares, J. and Wacziarg, R. (2001) "How Democracy Affects Growth," *European Economic Review* 45: 1,341–78.

Temple, J. (1999) "A Positive Effect of Human Capital on Growth," *Economic Letters* 65: 131–4.

Therborn, G. (1977) "The Rule of Capital and the Rise of Democracy," *New Left Review* 103, May–June: 3–41.

Todaro, M. P. (1977) *Economic Development in the Third World: An Introduction to Problems and Policies in a Global Perspective*, New York: Longman.

Tsebelis, G. (1995) "Decision Making in Political Systems: Veto Players in Presidentialism, Parliamentarism, Multicameralism and Multipartyism," *British Journal of Political Science* 25: 289–325.

Tullock, G. S. (1980) *Toward a Theory of Rent-Seeking Society*, College Station, TX: Texas Agricultural and Mechanical University.

UNCTAD (1994) *Foreign Investment Directory: The Developed Countries*, New York: United Nations Publications.

UNCTAD (1998) *Trade and Development Report*, New York: United Nations Publications.

UNCTAD (2000) *World Investment Report: Cross-Border Mergers and Acquisitions and Development*, New York: United Nations Publications.

UNCTAD (2001) *World Investment Report: Promoting Linkages*, Geneva: United Nations Publications.

UNDP (1998) *Human Development Report*, New York: Oxford University Press.

UNDP (1999) *Human Development Report: Globalization with a Human Face*, New York: Oxford University Press.

UNICEF (2000) *The State of the World's Children*, Geneva: United Nations Children's Fund.

UNICEF (2001) *The State of the World's Children*, Geneva: United Nations Children's Fund.

United Nations (1988) *Transnational Corporations in World Development: Trends and Prospects*, New York: United Nations Publications.

United Nations (1991) *Government Policies and Foreign Direct Investment*, New York: United Nations Publications.

United Nations (1992) *The World Investment Report: Transnational Corporations as Engines of Growth*, New York: United Nations Publications.

United Nations (1995) *The World Investment Report*, New York: United Nations Publications.

Valenzuela, S. J. and Valenzuela, A. (1978) "Modernization and Dependency: Alternative Perspectives in the Study of Latin American Development," *Comparative Politics* 10, July: 543–57.

Vanhanen, T. (1990) *The Process of Democratization: A Comparative Study of 147 States, 1980–1988*, New York: Crane Russak.

Vanhanen, T. (1993) "Construction and Use of an Index of Democracy," in Westendorff, D. and Ghai, D. (eds) *Monitoring Social Progress in the 1990s: Data Constraints, Concerns and Priorities*, Brookfield: Avebury.

Vanhanen, T. (1997) *Prospects of Democracy: A Study of 172 Countries*, London: Routledge.

Vanhanen, T. (2000) "A New Dataset for Measuring Democracy, 1810–1998," *Journal of Peace Research* 37, 2: 251–65.

Vanhanen, T. (ed.) (1992) *Strategies of Democratization*, Washington: Crane Russak.

Väyrynen, Raimo (ed.) (1999) *Globalisation and Global Governance*, Lanham, MD: Rowman and Littlefield.

Verdier, D. (1998) "Democratic Convergence and Free Trade," *International Studies Quarterly* 42: 1–24.

Vernon, R. (1971) *Sovereignty at Bay: The Multinational Spread of US Enterprises*, New York: Basic Books.

von Laue, T. (1987) *The World Revolution of Westernization: The Twentieth Century in Global Perspective*, New York: Oxford University Press.

Waldner, D. (1999) *State Building and Late Development*, Ithaca, NY: Cornell University Press.

Wallerstein, I. (1974) "The Rise and Future Demise of the World Capitalist System: Concepts for Comparative Analysis," *Comparative Studies in Society and History* 16: 387–415.

Warren, Bill (1981) *Imperialism: Pioneer of Capitalism*, New York: Knopf.

Waterbury, J. (1999) "The Long Gestation and Brief Triumph of Import-Substitution Industrialization," *World Development* 27, 2: 323–41.

Webster, A. (1995) "Modernization Theory," in Ayers, R. (ed.) *Development Studies: An Introduction Through Selected Readings*, Greenwich: Greenwich University Press.

Weede, E. (1981) "Three Dependency Explanations of Economic Growth: A Critical Evaluation," *European Journal of Political Research* 9: 391–406.

Weede, E. (1986a) "Rent Seeking, Military Participation, and Economic Performance in LDCs," *Journal of Conflict Resolution* 30, 2: 291–314.

Weede, E. (1986b) "Rent Seeking or Dependency as Explanations of Why Poor People Stay Poor," *International Sociology* 1, 4: 421–41.

Weede, E. (1996a) *Economic Development, Social Order, and World Politics: With Special Emphasis on War, Freedom, the Rise and Decline of the West, and the Future of East Asia*, Boulder, CO: Lynne Rienner.

Weede, E. (1996b) "Political Regime Type and Variation in Economic Growth Rates," *Constitutional Political Economy* 7: 167–76.

Weede, E. and Tiefenbach, H. (1981) "Some Recent Explanations of Income Inequality: An Evaluation and Critique," *International Studies Quarterly* 25, 2: 255–88.

Wei, S.-J. (2000) "Natural Openness and Good Government," Cambridge, MA: National Bureau of Economic Research.

Weiner, M. and Huntington, S. P. (eds) (1987) *Understanding Political Development*, Boston: Little, Brown.

Weingast, B. R. (1993) "Constitutions as Governance Structures: The Political Foundations of Secure Markets," *Journal of Institutional and Theoretical Economics* 149, 1: 286–311.

Weingast, B. R. (1997) "The Political Foundations of Democracy and the Rule of Law," *American Political Science Review* 91, 2: 245–63.

Weitzman, M. L. (1993) "Capitalism and Democracy: A Summing Up of the Arguments," in Bowles, S., Gintis, H., and Gustafsson, B. (eds) *Markets and Democracy: Participation, Accountability and Efficiency*, Cambridge: Cambridge University Press.

Willett, S. (2001) "Introduction: Globalization and Insecurity," *Institute for Development Studies Bulletin* 32, 2: 1–12.

Williamson, J. G. (1997) "Globalization and Inequality Past and Present," *World Bank Research Observer* 12, 2: 117–35.

Williamson, J. G. (ed.) (1994) *The Political Economy of Policy Reform*, Washington, DC: Institute for International Economics.

Wills, G. (ed.) (1982) *The Federalist Papers*, New York: Bantam.

Wimberley, D. and Belo, W. (1992) "Effects of Foreign Investment, Exports and Economic Growth on Third World Food Consumption," *Social Forces* 70: 895–921.

Wintrobe, R. (1990) "The Tinpot and the Totalitarian: An Economic Theory of Dictatorship," *American Political Science Review* 84, 3: 849–71.

Wittfogel, K. A. (1957) *Oriental Despotism: A Comparative Study of Total Power*, New Haven, CT: Yale University Press.

Wittman, D. (1995) *The Myth of Democratic Failure: Why Political Institutions Are Efficient*, Chicago: University of Chicago Press.

World Bank (1992) *The World Development Report: Development and the Environment*, New York: Oxford University Press.

World Bank (1995) *The World Development Report: Workers in an Integrating World*, New York: Oxford University Press.

World Bank (1996a) *The World Development Report*, New York: Oxford University Press.

World Bank (1996b) *The World Development Report: From Plan to Market*, New York: Oxford University Press.

World Bank (2000) *World Development Indicators 2000* (CD), Washington, DC: World Bank.

World Bank (2001) *World Development Indicators* (CD-ROM), Washington, DC: World Bank.

World Bank (2002a) *Globalization, Growth, and Poverty: Building an Inclusive World Economy*, Oxford: Oxford University Press.

World Bank (2002b) *The World Development Report: Building Institutions for Markets*, Oxford: Oxford University Press.

Index

For Product Safety Concerns and Information please contact our EU
representative GPSR@taylorandfrancis.com
Taylor & Francis Verlag GmbH, Kaufingerstraße 24, 80331 München, Germany

www.ingramcontent.com/pod-product-compliance
Lightning Source LLC
Chambersburg PA
CBHW050525270326
41926CB00015B/3073

9 781138 810747